Praise for *Build Better Slide Decks*

"Andrew Quagliata explains in crystal-clear terms how you can maximize the value of your slide decks, whether you are using them for live presentations, discussion catalysts, or detailed textual reports. You'll learn a systematic approach to analyzing audience, planning content, organizing a coherent story line, and modifying information density. Whether you are a student or a business practitioner, *Build Better Slide Decks* will help you achieve your goals."

— *Daphne A. Jameson, Professor Emerita,*
Management Communication, Cornell University,
SC Johnson College of Business and Past President,
Association for Business Communication

"*Build Better Slide Decks* brings Quagliata's real-world experience to the page in a way that's approachable, actionable, and guaranteed to sharpen your communication. This book belongs in every professional's toolkit."

— *Samay Bansal, Chicago Booth MBA Candidate*
and Former Business Analyst, McKinsey & Company

"*Build Better Slide Decks* distills presentation strategy into a clean, intuitive framework. Since incorporating these tactics into my day-to-day at Google, I've been weaving much more intentional storytelling through data—and it all comes together more cohesively. A must-read for any professional who wants their slides to land harder, look sharper, and tell a story that sticks."

— *Adam Saks, Senior Digital Strategy Lead, Google*

Want help bringing these ideas to your team?

Many of the principles in this book come from workshops I've led with professionals across industries—from hospitality leaders to investment managers. If your team would benefit from applying these ideas together, I offer virtual and in-person sessions tailored to your goals.

Participants walk away with tools to:

1. Clarify and sharpen the message behind every slide.

2. Build professional decks more quickly and with greater confidence.

3. Make smarter decisions about text, visuals, and layout.

4. Communicate strategy, data, and recommendations more effectively.

Here's what past workshop participants have said about the experience:

- "Andrew gave us a rare opportunity to step back, reflect, and align on how we use slide decks across the organization. The session sparked changes that continue to shape how we communicate."

- "Everything in this workshop was applicable to my role. The tools were practical, easy to understand, and ready to use the next day."

- "This is one of the few meetings in recent memory where I walked away having truly learned something valuable. I'll use these insights for the long term. Our day together was incredibly beneficial."

- "I really enjoyed Andrew's presence and his encouraging way of making space to practice. I walked away with tools that not only improved my communication but changed how I think about it."

To learn more, please visit SlideDeckBook.com.

BUILD BETTER SLIDE DECKS

Create Sharper Slides, Stronger Stories, and Standout Presentations

ANDREW B. QUAGLIATA, PHD

THIRD
PILLAR
PRESS

CONTENTS

FOREWORD

Who says old dogs can't learn new tricks?

Toward the close of a 40-plus-year career helping students and clients communicate effectively in the workplace, I've learned something new. And so can you.

You should read *Build Better Slide Decks* for two main reasons. First, your professional credibility may be on the line every time you share a slide deck. Second, no other resource offers an approach to slide decks as thoughtful and practical as this one.

This book delivers significant value—especially if, like many professionals, you're largely self-taught when it comes to workplace communication. Even if you've had formal training, it likely focused on text-heavy documents like emails and reports. And if you've received any guidance on slides, it probably emphasized how to support a live presentation—as if you're a "sage on the stage."

But slide decks are more than presentation aids. In many industries, they are among the most important documents you create. Their quality affects not only how well you communicate but also how others assess your thinking. Audiences will judge how well you organize data, surface conclusions, and support recommendations. They'll draw inferences about your analytical abilities and your overall professionalism.

Andrew Quagliata has spent two decades teaching management communication, researching how slide decks are used in practice, and helping professionals sharpen their message. In this book, he distills that experience into a clear, systematic process for planning, producing, and polishing decks that work.

The book makes two major contributions to the field. First, it offers a comprehensive framework that reflects how slide decks function across a range of real-world situations. Unlike most resources—which focus either on visual aids for oral presentations or dense stand-alone reports—this book addresses the full spectrum. It equips you to make smart decisions about what kind of deck to create, how to balance visuals and text, and how to design each slide with purpose.

Second, the book introduces an actionable approach to managing information density—one of the most overlooked yet critical factors in slide design. By focusing on two key metrics—information chunks and word count—Andrew gives you tools to assess and adjust how much content appears on each slide. These metrics help you tailor your deck to the situation, whether you're creating a live presentation, a leave-behind document, or something in between. With these metrics, you'll reduce clutter, sharpen focus, and create decks that are easy for your audience to scan, absorb, and act on.

Although *Build Better Slide Decks* is written for practitioners, its insights extend to academic contexts as well. Business students will gain a strong foundation in a form of communication central to many careers, especially in consulting and finance. Faculty, too, will benefit— from rethinking assignments to better prepare students for the demands of the workplace.

If you want to create slide decks that communicate clearly, influence decisions, and reflect your best thinking, this book will serve you well. It will help you meet your audience's needs—and, when it matters most, exceed their expectations.

Andrew Quagliata's *Build Better Slide Decks* won't provide you with the workplace equivalent of any new dog tricks. But it will provide you with something more valuable: a disciplined and systematic way to think about the slides you create and the stories you want your decks to tell.

> — *Craig Snow, Senior Lecturer, Management*
> *Communication, Cornell University, SC Johnson*
> *College of Business, Coauthor of* Guide to Report Writing

INTRODUCTION

Lynne had presented to the audit committee for years. As the senior vice president of finance at a large financial services firm, she took pride in delivering clear, transparent reports that reflected the financial health of the business. Yet, as she wrapped up her latest year-end presentation, she heard only silence.

"Any questions?" she prompted, scanning the room. The five committee members exchanged brief glances, then shook their heads.

"No questions? Let's move on to the next agenda item."

Walking back to her office, Lynne couldn't shake the feeling that something was wrong. She had seen this committee through regulatory changes, market shifts, and periods of financial uncertainty. But lately, their engagement seemed to be waning. Fewer questions. Less discussion. More rubber-stamping. It gnawed at her.

Lynne and her team had fulfilled their responsibilities. They produced accurate, detailed financial reports that ensured compliance and offered full transparency. But an unengaged audit committee posed a risk. These individuals were meant to provide oversight, to hold leadership accountable, and to safeguard the firm's financial health. If they were not actively contributing, how could they carry out their responsibilities?

Lynne had noticed two concerning patterns. First, committee members were asking fewer questions during the meetings. Second, when they did ask, the questions were often basic: the kind that should have been answered if they had read the reports.

She decided it was time to try a new approach. Rather than send another dense packet filled with pages of text and tables, she worked with her team to rethink how they communicated. For years, they had delivered thick reports that landed on desks with a heavy thud.

But what if they told the story differently? What if, instead of walls of text, they used a slide deck—something visual and easy to digest?

They replaced the 20-page document with a medium-density slide deck. Each slide told a story—using clear headings and visual evidence to support key insights. Financial trends were shown in charts rather than buried in footnotes. Key risks were highlighted up front. Supporting details were easier to skim.

Ten days before the next meeting, Lynne's team sent the updated materials. Then they waited.

When the committee members arrived at the meeting, Lynne immediately sensed a difference. One of the quietest members walked in holding a printed copy of the deck, covered in handwritten notes. Another had flagged several slides with questions. Once the meeting started, the conversation was more substantive than it had been in years. The committee moved beyond surface-level inquiries to discuss real issues, emerging risks, strategic priorities, and long-term goals.

Afterward, the committee chair sent Lynne a note: "Great meeting. Best discussion we've had in a long time."

Beyond improving engagement, the new format helped the committee fulfill its role more effectively. With clearer insights, members were better equipped to ask deeper questions, spot red flags, and provide real oversight.

Even the most diligent professionals can become passive when faced with dense reports that demand too much effort to unpack. The traditional financial packet buried the most important ideas in long paragraphs.

The new slide deck helped committee members grasp the story behind the numbers by bringing those insights to the surface and making them faster to find and easier to act on. And the change in the way the information was communicated resulted in better decision-making.

Lynne's experience reflects a broader change. Across industries, slide decks have become the tool professionals use to shape how decisions are made, strategies are formed, and teams are aligned. Whether you're an analyst, manager, educator, or executive, chances are you've used a slide deck to communicate your most important ideas.

Lynne's story is one example of a challenge that many others face. Professionals are producing more slide decks than ever, yet many of those decks fail to achieve their purpose. That's what led me to write this book.*

Why This Book and Why Me?

I never set out to become an expert on slide decks. But for more than twenty years, I have found myself working with slide decks in every aspect of my professional life.

My path started with degrees in professional and technical communication and an MBA. I began my career in higher education and finance, where I created and reviewed hundreds of presentations. Some were effective. Others made it harder to move ideas forward.

Along the way, I began teaching business communication on the side and discovered how much I enjoyed helping others make their ideas clearer and more compelling. That interest eventually led me back to school for a PhD in organizational communication, where I researched how people process information and how messages influence decisions. Most of the ideas in this book are grounded in that research. What I've done here is translate what scholars have learned about cognition and influence and apply it to one of the most widely used tools in the modern workplace: the slide deck.

For more than ten years now, I've taught management communication to business students at Cornell University. I've coached thousands of students, many of whom have gone on to work at firms like McKinsey, J.P. Morgan, and Hilton. They have tested these techniques in high-stakes meetings and shared valuable feedback with me that has

---

* The stories in this book are based on real experiences. Names, roles, and organizations have been changed to protect privacy.

helped refine what I teach. I also created Cornell's annual Hospitality Pitch Deck Competition, where students learn to develop their ideas and structure them into compelling presentations that resonate with industry decision-makers.

Beyond the classroom, I developed an online course through eCornell titled *Building Compelling Slide Decks and Reports* that helps professionals from around the world improve how they use slides to inform and persuade. I've worked directly with organizations trying to get better at telling their story—whether to investors, clients, boards, or internal teams. And I've conducted and presented multiple research studies on how publicly traded companies use slide decks to communicate, helping to ground my teaching in current business practice and data.

This book brings together everything I've learned: the classroom insights, the consulting and coaching experiences, the research, and the feedback from professionals who put these ideas into practice. My goal is simple: to help you create sharper slides, stronger stories, and standout presentations.

Let's begin by defining what I mean by *slide decks*, determining when to use them, and exploring how they are being used in professional settings today.

What Is a Slide Deck?

A slide deck is a tool for communicating ideas visually. Created with presentation software, a deck is a series of slides, typically in landscape orientation, that organizes information in a way that is easy to scan, absorb, and act on. Most workplace decks use PowerPoint or similar software such as Keynote or Google Slides.

Unlike traditional documents, decks rely on visual elements to clarify and support key points. Whether displayed in a conference room, presented in a virtual meeting, or read alone at a desk, a well-made slide deck breaks down complex information into key ideas people can quickly understand and use.[1]

Critics like Edward Tufte argue that slide presentations have become a crutch, reducing complex ideas into bullet points and slick graphics that obscure clear reasoning. In his influential essay *The Cognitive Style of PowerPoint*, he describes the medium as contributing to a degraded form of communication.[2]

And while Amazon received widespread attention when it banned PowerPoint in favor of beginning meetings with a silent reading of a six-page memo followed by a discussion, slide decks remain the go-to tool when professionals need to communicate information before, during, and after meetings.[3]

Contrary to some arguments that suggest slide decks encourage superficial thinking and presentation over substance, they are not inherently good or bad. Their effectiveness depends on how they are created and used.

Although presentation software has been around since the late 1980s, slide decks are still a relatively new way of communicating. Compared to written formats like letters, memos, and formal reports, which have evolved for more than a century, slide decks are still maturing. They emerged in practice, shaped by the needs of working professionals, not by scholars or writing instructors. As a result, most professionals never learned how to create them effectively.

This book aims to fill that gap.

When Should You Use a Slide Deck?

I'm writing a whole book about slide decks, so it might surprise you to learn that I don't think you should always use one.

Sometimes, an email is more appropriate. Sometimes, a quick phone call does the trick. And sometimes, a well-written memo is the clearest way to lay out a complex case.

Slide decks are especially useful in two situations:

- **When your message is visual**: If you're sharing a trend, comparing options, or making a case with data, visuals often work better than text. A good slide deck lets people see the story, not just read about it.

- **When your audience expects one:** In many organizations, slides are the standard format for updates, proposals, and pitches. When precedent favors a deck, creating one can help you align with expectations and simplify your decision about when to use one.

If your message needs visuals and your audience is accustomed to slide decks, you've got the green light. If not, pause and ask, Would another format work better?

This book will help you use slide decks well, and it will also help you know when not to use them at all.

How Did Slides Become the Standard
Way to Share Ideas at Work?

The way we communicate at work slowly evolves. Because so many of us may feel that we don't have enough time to accomplish all our tasks and may be suffering from information overload, speed and efficiency become more important. Slide decks with one idea per slide help audiences find the most important information quickly and process it easily.

The highly visual nature of slide decks helps explain why they have become so dominant in the modern workplace. Humans process visuals easier than text, and people remember images better than words.

Modern use of slide decks can be traced to when Microsoft acquired PowerPoint in 1987.[4] Shortly after, PowerPoint was bundled with Microsoft Office, and the corporate adoption of PowerPoint skyrocketed. Within the decade, using slides as we know them today became standard business practice. While presentation software was initially developed to design slides to support a live presentation, companies quickly found other ways to use it.

Consulting firms: Consultants saw an opportunity to transform traditional written reports into slide decks that could stand alone. Instead of lengthy reports filled with paragraphs and occasional charts and tables, firms like McKinsey, Boston Consulting Group (BCG), and Bain & Company began delivering insights in slides decks where each slide functioned like a report section. Slide decks also made it easier to repurpose content across projects, allowing consultants to reuse and adapt individual slides rather than reworking entire documents. Accounts from former consultants suggest that by the late 1990s, client deliverables were often in the form of a slide deck rather than a traditional (Word-based) report.

Startups: Simultaneously, entrepreneurs began using pitch decks as the standard way to raise capital. Many companies that eventually went public used pitch decks as part of the presentations that led to their initial public offerings (IPOs).

Publicly traded companies: By the early 2000s, investor relations professionals began reporting their quarterly earnings with slide decks. When the US Securities and Exchange Commission (SEC) implemented the "Fair Disclosure" regulation in 2000, mandating that all publicly traded companies disclose material information to all investors simultaneously, presentations with slides became an easy way to distribute information to institutional and retail investors. Around the same time, as internet bandwidth improved, it became common practice for public companies to webcast earnings calls, and these calls were often supplemented with slide decks.[5]

In each of these situations, slide decks were used to support live presentations, but they also had a larger purpose. They often functioned as something an audience might read before a live meeting, a handout an audience might look at during a meeting, and often a valuable reference after a meeting for those who attended and especially those who were not able to attend.

How Are Slide Decks Used Today?

Today, if a group of professionals gathers to share an idea, learn something new, or make a decision, there's a good chance a slide deck is involved.

From classrooms to conference rooms, boardrooms, war rooms, and virtual meeting rooms, slide decks are the tool professionals rely on:

- A manager presenting a quarterly update to align their team on strategy
- A sales leader pitching a new client, hoping to land a million-dollar deal
- An educator guiding students through topics, from art history to zoology
- A healthcare professional training new staff in a life-saving procedure
- A government official briefing stakeholders on a policy change

As you can see, from corporate boardrooms to nonprofit fundraising meetings, from job talks to TED-style talks, if there's a message to deliver, chances are someone's building a slide deck to do it.

But here's the problem: Most slide decks are ineffective.

Some lack a clear purpose, leaving audiences wondering, "Why am I here?" or "Why am I reading this?" Others are poorly adapted to the needs of their audience, packed with irrelevant details. Many are unstructured, bouncing between ideas without a clear thread. And far too often, slides are so cluttered with information that the main message gets lost.

We rely on slide decks to make decisions, shape careers, and define strategies, but most of us have never been taught how to build one effectively, and there's insufficient guidance on how to do it well.

That's where this book comes in.

This book isn't about how to use PowerPoint. You'll find no shortage of tutorials for that and let's be honest, a tech-savvy middle schooler could probably teach you faster than I can.

This book is about how to *communicate effectively* using presentation software.

There are books on how to prepare keynote presentations. There are books about how to write business reports. There are even books on how to prepare workplace presentations.

The problem with how most books address slide decks is that they assume there is just one right way to make them. They assume every deck should follow the same rules, no matter how it will be used. But that's not how real workplaces work.

Most people don't have time to create one version of a deck for presenting live and another for reading later. So, they try to make one deck that does it all. And instead, it does nothing well. It's too dense for a live audience or too vague for someone reading solo.[6] Slide decks aren't the problem; it's how we use them.

This book tackles that challenge head on.

Different situations call for different levels of detail. Sometimes a deck is meant to be seen, not read—a visual aid to accompany a presentation. At other times, a deck needs to accompany a discussion in a meeting. Sometimes a deck has to stand completely on its own—a document that readers can absorb without you in the room. And you may even need a deck that serves all three purposes. That's the most difficult balance to get right. But it's possible if you understand how to adjust the density to match the situation.

This book will help you get that decision right. Instead of treating all decks the same, you'll learn how to plan, produce, and polish the right slide deck for any workplace situation.

Before we dive into the main content of this book, let's put your slide deck instincts to the test. I've created a quick self-assessment for you to complete. No pressure. No grades. Just a fun way to see where you stand before we get started. You can take the quiz now at SlideDeckBook.com.

PART I

PLANNING YOUR SLIDE DECKS

When preparing a slide deck, you may find it difficult to resist the temptation to open your preferred software and start producing slides. Adding new slides and placing content into them can feel productive. However, doing so is like cooking a complex dish without a recipe. Throwing ingredients in a pot might feel productive, but without a clear vision of the final dish, you could end up with a mess instead of a masterpiece.

Why do we so often begin producing without planning? Our brains love the feeling of progress. Each time we create a new slide, we get a small hit of dopamine, the chemical that rewards us for accomplishments. It's the same chemical that makes us feel good when we cross items off a to-do list or hit "send" on an email. But dopamine doesn't care about long-term outcomes. It just rewards us for doing something.

Research on task management has shown that, when faced with a variety of tasks, people often complete easier tasks first to feel productive, even though harder tasks may benefit us more in the long run.[1]

Planning doesn't give us the same instant reward. Planning engages the prefrontal cortex—the part of the brain responsible for long-term thinking and decision-making.

Your brain might reward you for jumping to the producing section of the book, but you should give the planning section a shot. Because without planning, you risk the following:

- **You create irrelevant and unfocused content.** Without clearly defining your goals up front, you might end up with a deck that doesn't answer the core question your audience cares about.

- **Your audience struggles to connect with your message.** When you skip the step that helps you to understand the audience's needs, you may end up including information that doesn't resonate with them and omitting information that they may need.

- **Your slide deck feels disorganized.** Without a logical structure, your audience may have trouble following your argument.

- **Your slide deck fails to meet expectations.** Without thinking through your audience's preferences, your deck might be too long, too dense, or inappropriate for the context.

And perhaps most frustrating of all, you may waste time creating content you don't use. Producing slides before you plan often leads to unnecessary slides, repeated revisions, or reworking of major sections. Even worse, it can result in an unclear story that leaves your audience confused. All this adds up to wasted effort and issues that planning could have avoided.

When you skip the planning stage, every misstep compounds into wasted time and effort. Let's begin by understanding foundation principles (chapter 1), defining what matters (chapter 2), mapping the structure of your story (chapter 3), and considering the information density of the deck you plan to create (chapter 4).

Understand
Foundation Principles

Jason glanced at the clock. Just after nine. Time to begin.

A junior product manager at a fast-growing consumer tech company, he was presenting to the executive team for the first time. He'd spent hours pulling data, compiling updates, and assembling his slides. He clicked to his first slide: two paragraphs of text in size 12 font. Then he turned toward the screen and started reading. Word for word.

Slide 2: a wall of bullet points.

Slide 3: a chart so dense it looks like it was designed by NASA.

By slide 5, one executive was checking her watch. Another scrolled through email. By slide 9, the VP of product leaned forward and said, "Can we skip ahead to the takeaways?"

Jason's face flushed. He glanced at the screen and scrolled through 27 more slides, most of them crammed with details no one had asked for and no one would remember.

The final slide appeared: a blurry stock photo and "Any questions?" in Comic Sans.

No one responded. Everyone in the room had already moved on—to their next meeting, their next email, their next coffee.

What went wrong?

The issue wasn't the information; it was the way it was presented. Too much text. No clear structure. No regard for how busy professionals process information. Jason seemed to have been working from a faulty set of assumptions about communication.

Before you begin building your next deck, let's unpack the foundation principles so you don't make the same mistakes.

Start with the goal, not the tool. Don't prepare a slide deck unless you have a good reason for choosing to prepare a deck.

You may be surprised that a book about slide decks would begin by asking you to question whether, in fact, you need a slide deck. But not every communication situation calls for a slide deck.

Consider whether a slide deck is necessary to accomplish your goal. For instance, instead of displaying slides while you present, you could present without slides. If you are preparing a report, instead of writing the report with presentation software, you could prepare a traditional text-based report.

Preparing a slide deck entails a variety of costs that you can minimize if you choose not to prepare one. If you can accomplish your communication goal without a deck, you will have saved yourself (and possibly others) the time it takes to prepare an effective deck. The greater cost of building slides is what else you could have done with that time. Every hour spent preparing a slide deck is an hour not spent on other tasks.

Are you willing to spend the time needed to prepare your slide deck to get it right—to ensure you don't leave out key details, choose the wrong words, or risk that your readers misunderstand or reject your ideas?

Try This with AI

Test whether you even need a slide deck. *Prompt:* "I'm preparing to communicate [brief situation]. What are some reasons to use a slide deck in this situation and what alternatives might be more effective?"

Attention is not guaranteed. Unlike your fourth-grade teacher who was likely to give you their full attention when you presented and read every word you wrote, you can't expect the same from a business audience. Just because you've prepared a slide deck doesn't mean your audience will listen to your presentation, participate in a discussion you're leading, or read what you send them.

Audiences engage with content with a practical purpose. Every person who engages with your slide deck is consciously or unconsciously looking for value—an insight, a recommendation, an answer to a pressing question. Your audience expects something useful in return for this time. If they're an executive, they might need to decide whether to approve a proposal. If they're a prospective client, they might be weighing whether to invest in your service. If they're a project team, they may need clarity on the next steps.

Busy professionals process information quickly. Your audience is likely to scan, filter, and extract what's relevant so they can get what they need as quickly as possible. This means that *how* you present information matters just as much as *what* you present. If your content is buried in long explanations, your audience will either miss key insights or tune out entirely. But if your content is laid out effectively, your audience will grasp your message faster and retain it longer.

Brevity is not the highest-level virtue. Your slide deck should be long enough to accomplish your goal and meet your audience's expectations, but no longer. One slide or 100 slides—it doesn't matter. The right number of slides is as many as necessary, but no more.

Just because you can, doesn't mean you should. Presentation software gives you an excessive amount of freedom—and that's the problem. The software allows you to use a template that looks like it was designed in 1998. It provides you with an unlimited number of color choices and so many shapes! You can use a different typeface on every slide—maybe mix in Comic Sans, Curlz MT, and Papyrus for variety. You can animate text to bounce, flip, whip, or drop onto the screen. You can insert transitions to morph, airplane, and vortex your way through your deck. Remember this: Just because presentation software lets you do something doesn't mean it's a good idea.

Effective communication is a learnable skill. You don't need a graphic design degree to create a slide deck that informs others, shapes a discussion, or influences leaders. You don't need an eye for typography or an instinct for color palettes. A well-prepared deck helps your audience understand and act on your message. And the best part? Anyone can learn how to do it.

Slide Deck Myths & Truths

Here are four false beliefs that lead even the brightest people astray.

Myth #1: There's a correct number of slides in a deck.

The number of slides doesn't determine the quality of the presentation. A 30-minute talk with five slides can be wonderfully clear or a confusing mess. I've seen five-minute presentations with 30 slides run seamlessly, and others that felt like a blur. If you begin by asking, "How many slides should the deck have?" you are asking the wrong question.

Myth #2: A deck that has a visually inviting design is an effective deck.

Great design enhances clarity. It doesn't replace it. A well-designed but poorly structured deck will confuse the audience, and buried or omitted main points will frustrate your audience. No amount of visual finesse or help from AI tools that promise beautiful slides can fix unclear ideas or missing logic.

Myth #3: Slide decks are only for presentations.

Not always. Some decks support live talks, some serve as discussion tools, and others are designed to be read. Treating every deck as a presentation on slides ignores the versatility of slide decks as a communication tool.

Myth #4: Experts build great decks quickly.

Most great decks don't start great. They get there through planning, producing, and polishing. If a deck feels effortless to the audience, it's likely because the person who made it put a lot of thought into making the ideas easy to follow.

The following truths reflect what experienced communicators know and what this book will help you practice.

Truth #1: To prepare an effective slide deck takes time.

Effective communicators invest more time when the stakes are higher—and they know when a quick-and-dirty version is enough.

Truth #2: A great deck evolves.

Even skilled and experienced communicators rarely generate a first-time, perfect final draft. Especially for longer, complex, sensitive, nonroutine, and high-stakes decks, effective storytellers let their messages evolve in stages.

Truth #3: The early stages are often frustrating.

Slide deck creation is rarely smooth. False starts are a normal part of the process.

Truth #4: Anyone can learn to prepare effective slide decks.

You don't need to be a graphic designer. You need a clear message, a thoughtful process, and a few key principles—which you will find in this book.

Chapter 1 Takeaways

- Start with your goal, not your tool. Don't default to creating a slide deck. Only use one if it's the best choice for your communication purpose.

- Every deck asks that your audience invest their time and attention. Respect their investment by offering insights—not just information.

- Busy professionals scan first and read later. Structure your content so they can find what matters most, quickly and with minimal effort.

- Brevity isn't always better. The right length for your deck is whatever it takes to support your message—no more, no less.

- Presentation software gives you too much freedom. Just because you can add animations, gradients, or ornate typefaces doesn't mean you should.

- Slide deck creation is a skill, not a talent. You don't need to be a graphic designer to create a clear, compelling deck; you just need a better process.

Now that you've seen the common pitfalls and possibilities of using slide decks, it's time to get more deliberate. Chapter 2 walks you through the core decisions that shape everything that follows: your purpose, your audience, and your content.

Define What Matters

Julia had just stepped into a new role as director of operations at a busy regional hospital. Her first major assignment was to present a strategic update to the hospital's executive team. Wanting to show she had a firm grasp of the department, she packed her slide deck with everything she thought they'd want to see—charts on patient throughput, details about staffing challenges, vendor delays, supply closet audits, even notes on a pilot project for meal service.

She walked into the meeting with 37 slides and began presenting. But fifteen minutes in, the chief operating officer leaned forward and asked, "Julia, I'm still not clear; what are you asking us to focus on?"

Julia froze. She had included data related to her primary responsibilities, but the presentation didn't have a clear purpose.

After the meeting, her mentor stopped by her office. "You gave them all the news," he said gently. "But what they needed were the headlines." He explained that while her data was solid, the deck lacked focus. The executive team wasn't sure what problem she was raising or what action she wanted them to take.

That conversation stuck with her. She realized the update had been informative, but it wasn't actionable. And while quarterly presentations gave her a regular platform, they were only useful if people walked away with direction.

Three months later, Julia returned for her next update. This time, she narrowed in on a single pressing issue: reducing emergency department bottlenecks before flu season surged. She framed the presentation around one question: *How can we improve patient flow in the next six weeks?* She then structured her slides to answer it directly.

The difference was immediate. Instead of getting lost in the weeds, the executive team discussed trade-offs, resource allocation, and next steps. The shift came from clarity of purpose. Julia took the time to define what mattered, and that clarity gave her audience something to focus on, react to, and act upon.

Before you begin writing slide headings and designing visuals, you need to understand the core of your message and the context for your deck. This chapter is about answering the fundamental questions that define your communication.

What's the purpose? Why are you creating this slide deck? What question does your audience need answered? What outcomes are you trying to achieve? Who is your audience, and what do they need from you? What constraints—such as time, space, or attention—will shape how you prepare and deliver your message?

If you skip this step in favor of the immediate gratification that comes from building slides, you risk overloading your audience or leaving them without a clear takeaway.

Defining what matters is about narrowing your focus. Like guardrails, it keeps your message from drifting off track. It's about creating the right message for a specific audience in the right situation. Get this step right and producing the deck will be easier. Skip it and producing the deck will be more difficult.

This chapter will guide you through the following:

- Defining your purpose for communicating
- Understanding your audience

- Accounting for practical constraints
- Planning your content

Define Your Purpose for Communicating

The purpose of your slide deck is the foundation from which everything else builds. The purpose answers the question: Why are you communicating?

You might communicate using a slide deck for many reasons. But in most cases, those reasons fall into one of four broader purposes: inform, update, persuade, or engage. Let's look at one example for each:

- To *inform* senior leadership of the findings from a market research study
- To *update* employees on the progress of the current strategic planning process
- To *persuade* the executive team to adopt a new initiative
- To *engage* department heads in a collaborative discussion about priorities for the strategic plan

Defining your purpose for communicating shapes many of the decisions that follow as you plan, produce, and polish your deck. Without a clear focus, your deck risks being unfocused and ineffective.

Inform

For many professionals, the most common purpose of a slide deck is to inform. These decks equip the audience with the information they need.

Summarize Research, Findings, or Data

- To inform clients about findings from an analysis of emerging markets
- To inform colleagues of the results of the most recent student satisfaction survey

Teach or Train

- To inform new advisors about advanced financial modeling techniques
- To inform employees about a new safety policy

Demonstrate

- To inform prospective clients of the firm's financial planning software through a live walkthrough
- To inform students how to register an event on campus using the new event registration system

Update

Like decks that inform, decks that update share information. But update decks provide a snapshot of progress or performance. They answer the question: What's happening? Where do things stand?

Report on Status

- To update leadership on the status of a client onboarding project
- To update department leaders on the status of a new performance management system

Report on Performance

- To update senior advisors on the performance of a newly launched investment fund
- To update institutional leadership on the performance of a fundraising campaign

Persuade

Some decks go beyond informing by attempting to change minds, influence decisions, or motivate action.

Advocate for a Proposal or Decision

- To persuade a client to transition from a traditional asset allocation model to a more diversified strategy
- To persuade university administration to establish an office of general counsel

Influence Decisions or Motivate Action

- To persuade a client nearing retirement to begin estate planning
- To persuade students to participate in a campus-wide festival

Sell or Market a Product, Service, or Idea

- To persuade a client to invest in a new tax-advantaged product
- To persuade senior leaders to consider a new student advising model

Engage

The purpose of a deck that engages is to facilitate collaboration. The deck serves as a tool to spark discussion, guide brainstorming sessions, or frame decision-making processes.

The deck helps create space for others to contribute and shape the outcome. They may include prompts or exercises that encourage active participation from the audience.

Facilitate Discussions

- To facilitate a discussion about intergenerational wealth transfer
- To facilitate a discussion among campus leaders about improving student retention rates

Support Decision-Making

- To help leadership decide about office leasing locations
- To assist the board of trustees in deciding on tuition adjustments

Guide Brainstorming

- To explore ways to improve the client service model
- To guide a department in brainstorming ideas for a new logo

Avoid Common Pitfalls

Understanding the purpose of your slide deck is the first step in the planning process. But even with a clear purpose in mind, three common pitfalls can derail your efforts:

- **Skipping the purpose check:** If you don't confirm your purpose with your audience before you begin preparing your deck, you may spend time creating slides that fail to deliver what your audience needs. Instead, take time early on to align with your stakeholders. A brief conversation or clarifying email can increase the chances that you are heading in the right direction.

  While this book is presented in a linear fashion, revisiting your purpose for communicating while preparing your slides is also a good idea. It's easy to lose sight of the purpose (and subsequently add unnecessary slides), so periodically think about the desired outcome and make sure your content stays aligned with your goals.

- **Combining too many purposes:** If you combine too many purposes as you prepare a deck, you may confuse your audience. Instead, you should consider what's most important and let that main purpose guide your decisions. You may also consider creating distinct sections in the deck for each purpose or creating two different decks. This issue is common when we try to prepare one deck for use with multiple audiences.

- **Misaligning purpose and audience expectations:** If the purpose you identify doesn't align with the needs of your audience, your communication may be ineffective. For example, if your audience is anticipating a clear update but you try to persuade them to take action, they may resist. Consider your audience's expectations of the situation and tailor your approach accordingly.

Determine the Governing Question

Another way to articulate your purpose for communicating is to identify the core question your deck needs to answer. My colleague Craig Snow calls this the *governing question.*

You can clarify your purpose for communicating by writing a governing question—a single, specific question your presentation or report needs to answer. Like a clear purpose statement, a governing question helps keep you focused and prevents your message from moving off track.

A governing question keeps your audience at the center of your planning activities. For example, if your purpose is to persuade the investment committee to accept your recommendations, the governing question your audience wants to answer is *Should we invest?*

A well-defined governing question acts like a filter for your content. As you develop your slide deck, the governing question allows you to evaluate each idea and ask, Does this help answer the question? If the answer is no, it's a sign that the content might be unnecessary. For example, detailed background information about a specific industry that your audience, composed of experienced investors, likely already knows might waste time or distract from the governing question, *Should we invest?*

The governing question for any communication varies depending on its purpose, whether the goal is to inform, persuade, update, or engage:

- Inform: What key information does the audience need?
- Update: What progress or performance metrics does the audience need?
- Persuade: How might you convince the audience to act or agree with a recommendation?
- Engage: How can this slide deck help facilitate discussion, decision-making, or idea generation?

Understand the Difference Between Purpose Statements and Governing Questions

The purpose statement and governing question help you determine *why* you are communicating and focus on *what* to communicate. To illustrate this relationship, here are examples of purpose statements paired with governing questions:

Purpose Statement: To inform senior leadership of the findings from a market research study.

Governing Question: What key insights from the market research study do the senior leaders need as we begin the strategic planning process?

Purpose Statement: To persuade the executive team to adopt a new initiative.

Governing Question: Why is this initiative the best choice to achieve our strategic goals?

Purpose Statement: To update employees on the progress of the current strategic planning process.

Governing Question: How has the strategic planning process advanced since the last employee update?

Purpose Statement: To engage department heads in a collaborative discussion about priorities for the strategic plan.

Governing Question: What priorities should the strategic plan reflect?

Sometimes a purpose statement provides all the direction you need, but for more complex or high-stakes communication, a governing question can force you to think more critically about what your audience truly needs. You may find that a purpose statement gives you a sense of the big picture, and a governing question helps you narrow the scope.

Understand Your Audience

Your audience should shape every decision you make about your slide deck.

Who are they? What do they need, know, and expect? This section will introduce a three-step process that will allow you to understand your audience better:

Step 1: Identify your audience

Step 2: Analyze your audience

Step 3: Confront the curse of knowledge

1. Identify Your Audience

The first step is to identify the individual or group of individuals who will be on the receiving end of your message. On the surface, identifying your audience seems like a straightforward task: Know who will be in the room or reviewing the deck. However, in practice, it's often more challenging.

Sometimes you'll create a slide deck specifically for an audience you know well, such as a team of executives, group of clients, or committee within your organization. In these cases, your audience is clear from the start and your focus shifts to planning how your message can fit their expectations.

Other times, you're asked to create a deck for an unfamiliar audience. You might receive vague instructions like "prepare a deck for senior leadership" or "put together slides for the client meeting" without knowing exactly who the audience will be. In these situations, it can help to gather more information, such as who will attend and what their roles are.

You may also have situations where you know your primary audience but not the secondary audience. For example, you might present to a department head, but their recommendations will be reviewed by an executive team you never meet. In this situation, you must identify who will hear or read your message firsthand but also anticipate who else might review your message.

2. Analyze Your Audience

To identify your audience isn't sufficient; you also need to consider how you can tailor your message to your audience, a process that may be complex.

Sometimes your audience comprises a diverse group with varying levels of expertise, competing priorities, or different decision-making powers. Imagine you're presenting a strategy update to the board of directors. Some members live and breathe financials, while newer members need more context to follow along. If you prepare a detailed financial analysis, you may lose half the room. If you oversimplify, you'll frustrate the experts. A one-size-fits-all approach won't work.

In these situations, consider designing your message for the individuals most central to your communication goal. Trying to please everyone can weaken your message. That doesn't mean you should ignore the rest of the audience, but your message should prioritize the people whose understanding, approval, or action matters most. If others need additional detail, background, or reassurance, you can address those needs with optional slides, examples, or follow-up materials.

Other times, the challenge isn't just who is in the room, but who influences the decision beyond the immediate audience. A department head might sit through your presentation, but the CFO or an external stakeholder might review the slides later before making the final call. That means your deck must serve multiple audiences, including those who experience it live and those who may encounter it later without your commentary.

As you analyze your audience, consider how you can frame your message to the specific people who will consume your message. *Framing* simply means deciding how to present your ideas in a way that makes sense to your audience. The same core message can land very differently depending on how you introduce it, what details you emphasize, and what examples you use. A skeptical audience requires a different approach than one that's likely to be receptive to your ideas. A high-level audience won't process your message the same way as one that expects a comprehensive breakdown of your ideas. Each insight you gather as you analyze your audience should help you adjust your message to make it more effective.

Analyzing your audience is about understanding what they think. As Stephen Covey once wrote, "Seek first to understand, then to be understood."[1]

As you prepare, consider these six factors to help you tailor your message to your audience. They aren't the only ones that matter, but they'll give you a strong foundation.

- **Needs:** What are they looking to get out of the presentation?
- **Knowledge:** How much do they already know?
- **Attitudes:** Are they skeptical? Enthusiastic? Resistant to change?
- **Goals:** What are they trying to accomplish?
- **Decision-making process:** What approach will they use to decide?
- **Communication preferences:** How do they prefer to listen, discuss, and/or read?

I'll describe each factor, then follow it with a *Framing in Action* section to help you apply the insight to your message.

Needs

Understanding the needs of your audience means recognizing what they expect to gain from your presentation. You may find it helpful to think of audience needs in four categories.

First, you should consider the *functional needs* or the job-to-be-done needs. If you're presenting to investors, they need enough data to assess risk. If you're presenting to leadership on a project, they need a clear picture of progress and roadblocks.

Second, *cognitive needs* focus on how your audience processes information. Some people need a step-by-step breakdown, while others prefer relatable stories. A slide full of numbers might appeal to someone who is data driven, while a case study might be better for a big-picture thinker.

Third, *emotional needs* are often more implicit. Is your audience likely to be skeptical and in need of reassurance? Might they be under pressure and in need of clarity? A team facing a major change might be listening less for details and more for cues that tell them, "Is this going to be okay?"

Finally, *contextual needs* are the external pressures that shape how your audience receives your message. Maybe your audience is constrained by corporate policies, industry regulations, or leadership expectations. Maybe they're relaying your ideas to someone else after your meeting? If so, your deck needs to carry the message on its own when you're not there to speak for it.

When your deck reflects what your audience truly needs, they're more likely to pay attention and walk away feeling you've added value.

Framing in Action: Ask yourself, what framing will make my message feel relevant to my audience's needs?

Try This with AI

Test your audience understanding. "Here's what I know about my audience: [insert details]. Based on this, what are the top three needs or questions they'll likely bring to my deck?"

Knowledge

Consider your audience's level of expertise from nonexpert to expert. Remember that intelligence doesn't always equal familiarity. Even highly capable audience members may be well-informed about some topics but less knowledgeable about others.

Your understanding of what your audience already knows should shape both the structure of your deck and the content you include:

- **Structure:** Where should you begin? A more novice audience may need some foundational framing, while an expert audience may prefer you jump straight to your insights.

- **Content:** How much detail is necessary? How much technical jargon is appropriate? What background information needs to be included or omitted?

Your understanding of your audience's knowledge can also shape the complexity of your explanations. Consider this example, which shows two different ways of explaining the same concept, each aligned to a different level of expertise.

- **Nontechnical:** Net Promoter Score (NPS) tells you how likely your customers are to recommend your company to others—it's a simple way to gauge customer loyalty.
- **Technical:** NPS is a metric derived from survey data that quantifies customer loyalty by subtracting the percentage of detractors from the percentage of promoters.

Framing in Action: To meet your audience where they are, avoid oversimplifying your message. Use analogies, visuals, or simplified terms to make your message accessible. Aim to accomplish your communication objective, not to impress.

Attitudes

If you've ever presented what you thought was a crystal-clear message only to be met with blank stares, you know that facts alone don't help you accomplish your communication goals. People don't receive information like empty containers waiting to be filled. Instead, they process your message through mental filters. These filters are deeply ingrained attitudes, beliefs, and values, and they shape how your audience interprets what you say. If your message clashes with these filters, your audience will resist it, ignore it, or reinterpret it in a way that aligns with what they already believe.

So, how do you figure out what those filters are? You can't read minds, but you can identify common patterns in how people think. Do they believe your message instinctively or require proof? How do they handle uncertainty and decision-making? Do they value continuity or disruption? What kind of evidence persuades them?

Skeptical vs. Trusting

Does your audience need convincing or just the right nudge?

Some audiences instinctively doubt what they hear, poking holes in arguments and demanding proof. Others lean toward trusting the source. If they believe in the messenger, they'll believe in the message. Persuasion expert Robert Cialdini identifies credibility and social proof as two of the biggest drivers of influence.[2] The more skeptical an audience, the more they need data, case studies, and independent validation before they buy in. The more trusting they are, the more they need to see alignment between your message and the values they already hold.

If you're pitching a new initiative to a skeptical finance team, you wouldn't want to start with vision. You might start with a case study from a competitor who's already succeeded in using this approach. But if you are pitching the same initiative to a leadership team that values innovation and trusts you, you might focus on how the idea aligns with the company's growth plans.

Risk-Averse vs. Risk-Tolerant

Does your audience want stability or a bold move?

Daniel Kahneman and Amos Tversky's prospect theory revealed that people hate losing more than they love winning.[3] This is why risk-averse audiences focus on stability and downside protection, while risk-tolerant audiences lean toward bold opportunities with high upside. The same information can trigger enthusiasm or anxiety, depending on how you frame it.

If you're presenting a new investment strategy to conservative clients, you should emphasize protection against market volatility and a history of steady returns. If your audience consists of venture capitalists (who don't typically care about slow and steady), you might emphasize how the investment strategy could lead to market domination and rapid growth.

Traditional vs. Forward-Looking

Does your audience value legacy or innovation?

Every time a new idea is presented, people respond at different speeds. Some welcome it, excited by the possibilities. Others resist it and question whether it's necessary or better than what's already working. In *Diffusion of Innovations*, Everett Rogers proposed that some people are early adopters, eager to experiment, while others wait until an idea is fully proven before even considering it. At the far end of the spectrum, traditionalists need compelling proof (or external pressure) before accepting change.[4]

In other words, some people ask, "How does this fit with what we've done before?" and others ask, "What's the new advantage this creates?"

A hospital considering a new diagnostic tool might have traditionalist doctors who need to hear how the tool fits into their existing methods of care, while progressive healthcare leaders want to hear about how it will keep them ahead of the curve and transform patient outcomes.

Data-Driven vs. Story-Driven

Does your audience want spreadsheets or stories?

Some people trust numbers; others connect through narratives, examples, and metaphors. In *Thinking, Fast and Slow*, Daniel Kahneman describes two systems of thinking. System 1 is intuitive and emotional, while System 2 is logical and analytical. Story-driven audiences rely more on System 1 thinking, making sense of information through emotional connections and examples. Data-driven audiences lean heavily on System 2 thinking, requiring numbers, research, and logical comparisons to feel confident in a decision.[5]

A corporate finance team may want to see five-year revenue projections. A nonprofit board considering a new funding initiative might be more persuaded by a powerful story about the impact of their donations.

These four spectrums aren't the only way to analyze your audience's attitudes, but they are a great place to start. They help you anticipate how people will filter your message and what objections might arise. Audiences are complex. Some are competitive, drawn to winning and outpacing the competition, while others value collaboration and shared success. Some crave structure and clear steps, while others prefer flexibility and big-picture thinking. The key is to recognize that your audience isn't a blank slate. They bring a perspective, and it's worth taking time to understand it during the planning stages.

Framing in Action: How can I frame my message in a way that aligns with the audience's existing viewpoints?

- **Skeptical:** Lead with proof (data, testimonials, results).
- **Trusting:** Lead with vision and alignment (how your message fits with their goals and existing beliefs).
- **Risk-Averse:** Frame your message as a safe, measured step forward rather than a leap into the unknown.
- **Risk-Tolerant:** Emphasize competitive advantages, potential gains, and the risk of doing nothing.
- **Traditional:** Connect your message to past successes and proven methods (frame it as an *evolution*, not a *revolution*).
- **Forward-Thinking:** Highlight how your idea differentiates your audience from competitors, disrupts the status quo, or future-proofs their business.
- **Data-Driven:** Lead with numbers, research, logical comparison (more chart than words).
- **Story-Driven:** Frame your message with personal stories, relatable scenarios, or emotional appeals.

Goals

Every audience member comes to a presentation with a goal. Maybe they need to learn something new, confirm something they already suspect, make a decision, or solve a pressing problem. If your slide deck doesn't help them accomplish that goal, it won't be effective, no matter how well-designed or well-delivered it is.

Some audience members may have implicit goals:

- What do they need to walk away with for this to be worth their time?
- What problems are they trying to solve?
- Are their goals aligned with yours, or will you need to find common ground?

A financial team reviewing an investment strategy may not need to hear a broad market overview; they likely want a clear recommendation with supporting evidence.

A university leadership team considering a curriculum redesign doesn't need a history lesson on higher education trends; they need insight into how the proposed curriculum will impact student success.

Let's consider four ways to analyze what your audience is hoping to accomplish. Uses and gratifications theory suggests that people engage with information based on what they want to accomplish—such as seeking knowledge, reinforcing beliefs, or solving problems. While originally developed to explain media use, the theory helps explain how workplace audiences also bring specific goals to each communication situation.[6]

Combining this idea with Kahneman and Tversky's prospect theory, we can better understand how people go about making decisions.

- **Are they seeking new information or insights?** Some audiences approach a communication situation with curiosity. They are looking to expand their understanding. When your purpose is to inform, it's likely your audience's goal is to explore.

- **Are they trying to confirm or challenge what they already believe?** Other audiences arrive with a preexisting point of view and they are looking for reinforcement or contradiction. The elaboration likelihood model explains that when people process new information, they either analyze it deeply (central processing) or skim for quick confirmation (peripheral processing).[7] In validation mode, audiences tend to engage in peripheral processing. They don't evaluate your message neutrally. Instead, they filter it through what they already believe.

- **Are they preparing to make a decision?** For some audiences, your message is about enabling a choice. Action-oriented audiences need insights and clear recommendations.
- **Are they trying to solve a problem?** Some audiences are trying to fix something ... a broken process, a stalled initiative, or an organizational challenge. Their focus is on finding a solution to an issue.

Which of these goals best describes your audience—are they exploring, validating, deciding, or solving? And based on that goal, what do they need most: context, proof, action steps, or solutions?

Framing in Action: How does your message connect to your audience's objectives?

- **Explore:** Build on ideas progressively.
- **Validate:** Anticipate assumptions, acknowledge counterpoints, and present evidence that either reinforces or challenges their perspective.
- **Act:** Identify choices and recommendations.
- **Resolve:** Define the problem, present the solution, and outline the next steps.

Decision-Making Process

If your audience needs to make a decision as a result of your message, you will want to consider the approach they take to decision-making. Individuals and groups rely on different decision-making styles to evaluate information, weigh alternatives, and commit to a course of action.

Researchers from the University of Colorado and University of Louisville identified five decision-making styles: rational, intuitive, dependent, avoidant, and spontaneous. Each style reflects habitual patterns in how people process choice, and each calls for a slightly different communication approach.[8]

Each of the following sections includes a brief description of the decision-making style, followed by a list of communication strategies that can support it.

Rational decision-makers follow a logical, systematic approach to making choice. They gather all relevant information, carefully evaluate alternatives, and rely on objective analysis before making a decision.

- Provide data and comparisons for evaluating options.
- Use step-by-step reasoning to support conclusions.
- Avoid overly vague or emotional appeals.

Intuitive decision-makers rely on instinct, experience, and pattern recognition. They often make decisions quickly, based on a sense of what feels right.

- Present the big picture before granular details.
- Use case studies and anecdotes.
- Structure content to emphasize insights over analysis.

Dependent decision-makers rely on others for advice before making a choice. They prefer to consult with experts, authority figures, or trusted colleagues and often defer to the consensus of the group.

- Highlight expert opinions, industry benchmarks, and authoritative sources.
- Include references to key stakeholders who support the proposed course of action.

Avoidant decision-makers tend to postpone, delegate, or avoid making decisions due to fear of making the wrong choice or uncertainty. They may need extra guidance, simplification, and reassurance before they commit to a decision.

- Simplify choices by reducing complexity and presenting manageable options.
- Reassure the audience by outlining risk mitigation strategies.
- Use timelines, deadlines, and next steps to encourage action.

Spontaneous decision-makers make quick decisions. They dislike lengthy deliberation and prefer to act fast with the information available.

- Get to the takeaways immediately (that is, no long-winded explanations).
- Make the recommendations concise.

Each of these styles relies on mental shortcuts, also known as *heuristics*, to simplify the decision process. Because our brains are wired to conserve energy, we often use heuristics to make choices without analyzing every detail. These shortcuts are efficient, but they also shape (and sometimes distort) how we process information.

Each style tends to favor different types of heuristics. Here's how these mental shortcuts typically emerge:

- **Rational:** Prone to confirmation bias—seeking out information that supports what they already believe
- **Intuitive:** Rely on instinct and pattern recognition, often drawing from past experiences
- **Dependent:** Tend to defer to authority, placing trust in experts or social consensus
- **Avoidant:** Influenced by default bias, choosing the easiest or most familiar option to avoid making a decision
- **Spontaneous:** Often affected by availability bias, anchoring, or recency effects, making quick choices based on what's top of mind

When I work with clients and ask about their own decision-making process—and how they think their audience decides—most people describe both themselves and their audience as rational decision makers. But research in behavioral economics and psychology suggests that although people believe they're making rational choices, they often aren't.

Decisions aren't made in a vacuum. No matter how logical or data-driven someone appears, their choices are often influenced by emotional, contextual, and social factors that shape how they receive and process information. Research by Kahneman and Tversky shows people tend to fear losses more than they value equivalent gains. This means risk aversion may override an otherwise rational cost-benefit analysis.

Context matters too. Time pressure, competing priorities, and organizational constraints can make individuals who may be reluctant to make decisions act impulsively or push an intuitive decision-maker toward a more systematic analysis.

Social factors like groupthink, hierarchy, and reputation can lead people to align with leadership expectations or defer to collective decision-making rather than follow their natural style.

When you recognize the factors that shape decisions, you can avoid the trap of overloading your deck with analysis while neglecting the emotional, contextual, or social factors that might drive the decision.

Framing in Action: What framing will best support how your audience makes decisions? To tailor your presentation effectively, consider how your audience approaches decision-making. Asking yourself the following questions can help:

- Which of these five decision-making styles best describes my audience?
- What kind of information will help them feel confident in making a decision?
- How can I present my message in a way that aligns with how they naturally process decisions?

Communication Preferences

Your audience likely has preferences about how they process information. If you are presenting live, you will want to consider how they listen. If you are facilitating a discussion, you will want to consider how they like to participate. And if you are sharing a slide deck that will be read, you will want to consider how your audience is likely to read the document.

To explore communication preferences in more depth, this section includes three models that will allow you to anticipate your audience's tendencies:

- **Listening preferences** describe how people prefer to receive and interpret spoken messages.
- **Discussion styles** reveal how individuals tend to engage in group conversations or collaborative problem-solving.
- **Reading approaches** highlight different ways readers navigate written messages.

Whether you are speaking, facilitating, or writing, these communication preferences should influence how you produce your slide deck.

Listening Preferences

Some people listen to build rapport. Others listen to get straight to the point. Some are hungry for details, while others are watching the clock. If you assume every member of a live audience listens the same way, you're bound to lose some of them during your presentation.

The Listening Style Profile, developed by Watson, Barker, and Weaver, identifies four distinct learning styles: People-Oriented, Action-Oriented, Content-Oriented, and Time-Oriented.[9] Knowing which one your audience leans toward can help you when planning your slide deck.

Each style is described here, followed by actionable strategies to help you communicate more effectively with listeners who tend to process information that way.

People-Oriented Listeners listen with their hearts first, heads second. They focus on emotions, relationships, and connection. A spreadsheet full of numbers? Boring. A compelling story about how those numbers affect real people? Now you've got their attention.

- Start with stories, examples, and personal anecdotes.
- Emphasize the human impact of your message.

If you plan to present a budget proposal to a leadership team that values relationships, don't just show cost savings. Instead, highlight how the new strategy improves team morale, supports employees, or strengthens customer relationships.

Action-Oriented Listeners don't show up for deep discussions or warm and fuzzy anecdotes. They want clear, structured, and efficient information. Their nightmare? A presentation that meanders.

- Start with the takeaway. Don't build up to it.
- Focus on what needs to happen next.

If you're planning to present a marketing strategy, begin with your recommendation and support that recommendation with evidence.

Content-Oriented Listeners love details. They want research, context, and a thorough breakdown of the topic. If you skim over the data, they may assume you're hiding something.

- Include well-researched content. Rather than just making claims, back them up.
- Evaluate issues from a variety of perspectives.
- Have extra details available, even if you don't put them all on the slides.

When you plan to present investment options to a content-oriented audience, a high-level summary won't be enough. Plan to share risk models, historical trends, and a detailed cost/benefit analysis.

Time-Oriented Listeners check their watches during a presentation. They value brevity, efficiency, and clear takeaways. If you ramble, you'll lose them.

- Trim the fluff. Every slide should have a purpose.
- Use time markers. For example, "In the next five minutes, we'll cover three reasons why …"
- Stick to the schedule. If you promise 20 minutes, don't take 30.

If you're planning a quarterly update to senior leaders, don't include unnecessary background information.

As you consider the listening preferences of your audience, you might ask two useful questions:

- Is my audience people focused or results focused?
- Does my audience prefer depth or efficiency?

Discussion Styles

Audiences are made up of individuals, and individuals show up to discussions in different ways. Some audience members love a good debate. Others prefer polite, measured conversation. Some will sit quietly until invited to speak, while others will dominate the room without hesitation. If you don't consider how your audience engages in discussion, you might design a slide deck that's too rigid for a lively group or too open-ended for an audience that prefers structure.

Individuals tend to reflect one of four dominant discussion styles: Passive, Aggressive, Passive-Aggressive, or Assertive. Each style reflects a different way of participating in a group conversation, and each one has implications for how you prepare your slide deck.

The following sections describe each discussion style and offer strategies for designing your slide deck to match.

Passive Audiences

Some audience members won't volunteer their thoughts easily. Maybe they're unsure of their expertise, hesitant to challenge authority, or simply prefer to process information quietly. This doesn't mean they're disengaged; it just means they're not going to fight for airtime.

If you plan to present to an audience who doesn't easily offer feedback, consider including discussion questions on your slides and sharing the questions in advance.

Aggressive Audiences

Some audience members jump in fast and won't hesitate to challenge what's on your slides. This isn't always a bad thing, but if left unchecked, it can create a one-sided discussion where only the loudest voices get heard.

If you're presenting to an opinionated audience, you can keep them focused by limiting the information on your slides and structuring your argument tightly. These adjustments help reduce the chances of your audience derailing the conversation.

Passive-Aggressive Audiences

Some audience members may not argue outright, but that doesn't mean they agree. They might nod along in the meeting, then challenge the plan later in private conversations. They value harmony in the moment but may withhold honest feedback until it's too late to address in real time.

Plan to provide this type of audience anonymous feedback channels, create slides that acknowledge potential concerns before they are voiced, and build in reflection time rather than expecting immediate buy-in.

Assertive Audiences

Some audience members communicate with confidence without being combative. They express their opinions openly and directly while remaining respectful of others. They aren't looking for conflict, but they won't shy away from it either. This is the type of audience you want for a productive discussion.

Plan to make space for both data and perspective. This audience appreciates evidence but also values well-reasoned opinions. Use your slides to structure the conversation and frame key questions, while leaving enough flexibility for meaningful dialogue.

Most audiences will include a mix of passive, aggressive, passive-aggressive, and assertive participants. To plan for mixed assertiveness styles, anticipate imbalances and design your slides to manage the various styles effectively:

- Use discussion slides to prevent aggressive voices from dominating. For example, "Let's hear from each team member before we move on."
- Provide reflection time to encourage passive communicators to contribute.
- Create anonymous input channels for audiences where passive-aggressive tendencies might keep people from voicing concerns openly.

Reading Preferences

Not everyone reads the same way. Some people skim. Some people read every word. If you design slides that demand too much mental effort, your audience may stop reading. However, if you design slides that don't include enough information, they might not take your content seriously. You can't assume your audience will read slides the way you do. Your challenge is to match your slide deck reading experience to your audience's reading needs.

Research by educational psychologists suggests that individuals have different capacities for processing new information. These capacities are affected by the complexity of the task, the conditions in which we process the information, and the limits of our working memory.

It's best to assume that skilled adult readers will attempt to process the least amount of information necessary to complete the task. In order to do so, they will focus on information they see as most relevant to the task and ignore information they see as less relevant.

High-Level Readers

Some people don't want to wade through paragraphs of text. These readers process information quickly by skimming and scanning. Skimmers rapidly move through text to grasp the main ideas. They want the essential information up front. Think of them as your "executive summary" readers. Scanners search for specific information in your deck. They move their eyes over the material to locate specific details. For example, a "numbers person" may jump to the cost/benefit analysis.

Advice: Use a table of contents, headlines, less text, bulleted lists, and more visuals.

Focused Readers

Focused readers want information, but the content must be well organized and easy to follow. They won't skip the details, but they don't want to work too hard. They may read some slides deeply and skim other slides.

Advice: Include clear sections, headlines, and supporting details.

Deep Readers

Deep readers seek a detailed understanding of the material. Some will read the deck from beginning to end and annotate along the way. Others will read the deck critically, analyzing, evaluating, and challenging the content as they read. These types of readers prefer full explanations and don't trust summaries without supporting evidence. If you oversimplify the content for them, they'll assume your analysis is weak.

Advice: Use details, more text, citations, and appendices.

In addition to considering your audience's reading preferences process, consider how much effort they're willing to invest. Researchers at the University of Michigan found that when information is hard to read, people will assume the task itself is more difficult, making them less likely to persist.[10] These findings suggest that if your audience perceives your deck as difficult to read, they will assume the task is more difficult and be less willing to read it.

The same study suggests that motivation plays a role in an audience's willingness to read. Those with high motivation will persist through difficult content, and those with low motivation will stop reading sooner.

To summarize, at least two factors shape how your audience interacts with your deck: their ability to process information and their willingness to read. So, as you plan your deck, ask yourself: Is my audience going to skim or read this deeply? And how motivated are they to read the content?

If you are unsure how your audience reads or their level of motivation, this book will teach you how to design slides that give readers the core message if they read the main idea, and if they dive into the details, they get enough substance (i.e., you will understand how to prepare a deck for readers at both ends of this spectrum). You'll also learn design strategies that will make your content appear easy to read so that, regardless of the motivation level, individuals will be more likely to keep reading.

Framing in Action: How can I frame this in a way that aligns with how my audience processes information?

Audience analysis is about understanding others. That means you shouldn't approach this stage in the planning process with a Golden Rule mentality. Rather than treating others the way you want to be treated, you should consider following the Platinum Rule: Treat others the way they want to be treated.

3. Confront the Curse of Knowledge

As you create your slide deck, you should keep in mind that it can be challenging to understand how others want to be treated. That's because we all suffer from the curse of knowledge. This is a cognitive bias we experience when we assume others have the background knowledge necessary to understand our message.[11]

To overcome the curse of knowledge when planning a slide deck, step into your audience's perspective and assume they know less about the topic than you do. A common mistake is to assume that what's obvious to you is obvious to them. This may lead you to create slides that are too complex, jargon heavy, or lacking in necessary context.

The challenge with audience analysis is that we overestimate our ability to understand other people's perspectives. In a series of 25 experiments, researchers from Ben-Gurion University, Northeastern University, and the University of Chicago found that when individuals tried to infer another person's thoughts or viewpoint, their predictions improved only slightly. In contrast, when people directly ask others for input, through conversation or specific questions, their accuracy increased significantly.[12]

These findings suggest that accurate understanding may require acquiring new information, not just an attempt to read people's minds or put yourself in their shoes.

Instead of guessing about your audience, attempt to seek direct input.

Test Your Assumptions

Here are five strategies, ranked from most to least effective, that can help you analyze your audience:

1. **Ask your audience.** The best way to understand your audience is to ask them directly. If you have access to your audience before preparing a slide deck, gather insights through informal conversations. For larger groups, surveys or questionnaires can reveal patterns in expectations, preferences, or pain points.

2. **Ask people who know your audience.** If direct access to your audience isn't possible, the next best thing is to speak with people who regularly interact with them. For example, an executive assistant may offer valuable insight into what a senior leader expects. Intermediaries often understand pain points, priorities, and decision-making styles.

3. **Ask others who are like your audience.** If neither direct nor secondhand input is available, gather input from people who resemble your audience in experience, role, or knowledge level. For example, I was once asked to deliver a presentation to a group of public-school superintendents, but I didn't have access to them in advance. I was able to secure a call with the superintendent of my hometown to understand some of the current challenges individuals in this role face so I could tailor my remarks more effectively.

4. **Ask others.** Even if someone isn't in your target audience, running your assumptions by a neutral third party can help you identify gaps in your thinking. A colleague, mentor, or friend can be helpful in this process.

5. **Make your best guess.** When none of the other options are possible, you'll have to make an educated guess. Do this strategically. Consider past presentations to similar audiences, structure your deck to allow flexibility by including optional slides that cover technical details, and plan to pause for questions so you can adjust in real time.

Once you've committed to gathering real audience insights, the next challenge is capturing that input in a way that can help you plan your slide deck. Asking vague or surface-level questions won't give you the depth you need, and listening passively may cause you to miss the most valuable takeaways. Instead, focus on two essential skills: asking the right questions and actively listening to what your audience is really saying.

Ask Questions That Reveal Useful Insights

The quality of the input you receive depends on the quality of the questions you ask. Don't merely ask broad questions like, "What do you want to hear about?" Instead, structure your questions to uncover specific needs, knowledge gaps, and preferences. Consider using these approaches:

- **Clarify expectations.** What is the most valuable takeaway you hope to get from this presentation?
- **Gauge knowledge level.** Would you prefer a high-level overview or more in-depth explanation?
- **Identify key concerns.** What's the main issue you're facing right now?
- **Understand decision-making style.** How do you anticipate deciding?

When speaking to intermediaries or similar audiences, adapt the questions to get secondhand insights.

- Do they prefer a presentation followed by questions and answers, or is this more likely to be a discussion?
- What kinds of questions does this audience typically ask during presentations?
- What do they tend to focus on most?

Listen for What Matters

Getting direct input is only valuable if you truly hear and interpret what your audience is trying to communicate. Active listening requires you to focus on patterns, priorities, and unspoken cues that reveal what's important to them. So how do you make sure you're really capturing what matters? Focus on three things:

- **Prioritize reoccurring themes.** If multiple people mention the same concern or request, you should be sure to address it in your deck.

- **Listen for hesitations.** Sometimes what people don't say is as telling as what they do say.
- **Ask follow-up questions when needed.** Check for clarity by asking, "Can you give me an example?"

Arrange a Time to Test Your Assumptions

The best way to gather input is through direct conversations, but before that can happen, you need to get in front of your audience. If you work in the same office as the people you are preparing the deck for, you might be able to informally stop by their office, but when that's not possible or you want to give your audience advance notice, you may need to send an email to request a face-to-face, virtual, or phone meeting.

Example Email

Hi, [Name],

I'm preparing a presentation on [topic] for [audience] and want to be sure it addresses their key concerns. Since you [have experience working with the group/understand their expectations], I'd really appreciate your insights.

Would you be available for a 15-minute conversation this week to help me understand what they already know, some of the challenges they face, and thoughts on the most effective way to present this information?

I am flexible on timing and happy to meet in person, over Zoom, or via a quick phone call.

Best,
[Your Name]

Email is a great way to request a conversation but not the best medium for listing all your questions and expecting thoughtful answers.

The more you replace assumptions with direct input, ask good questions, and listen actively, the better you will be able to tailor your content to your audience.

Identify Any Constraints That You Face

Two of the biggest constraints you face when preparing a slide deck are time and space.

Time

Time constraints come in two forms: how much time you have to prepare the deck, and if you are presenting, how much time you'll have to deliver it.

For example, a deck requested the night before a meeting imposes a very different constraint than one you've been asked to develop over several weeks. The shorter the timeline, the less opportunity you have to plan, produce, and polish your slides.

When you have time, you can follow the recommendations detailed in this book about aligning your message with your audience, gathering strong supporting materials, designing visually compelling slides, structuring a deck that flows, and getting feedback.

When time is short, prioritization is necessary. You don't have the luxury of testing designs, collecting comprehensive supporting material, or refining language. Instead, you must make quick decisions: What's essential? What's good enough? What do you have time to polish?

In these situations, prioritize what's essential. That might mean focusing on

- Clear structure over fine-tuned formatting
- Clear messages over customized data displays
- Essential support over detailed research

The second way time can be a constraint is when you present to a live audience. Most of us don't get to talk for as long as we want; we get the time the agenda allows. Maybe you're asked to give a one-slide update in under a minute, lead a 15-minute discussion, or present a budget proposal in 30 minutes. In some cases, you control the time constraint (i.e., you only need five minutes), and in others, it's imposed on you (i.e., you have exactly 10 minutes). Either way, how you manage that time shapes your audience's experience.

Audiences rarely mind if you end a little early. If you're given 10 minutes and you finish in eight, no problem. But if you finish in four minutes, it might seem like you haven't provided enough depth. And if you go over your allotted time, your audience may question your preparation or your respect for their time.

One more consideration: Time constraints don't always mean how long you should talk. They indicate how long you have the floor. A 20-minute presentation might include discussion and questions and answers. This means your actual speaking time is much shorter. In most workplace situations, people don't just want to be talked at; therefore, you should build in time for audience participation.

If a discussion is expected, build it into your timing. A deck that takes 10 minutes when rehearsed might take 15 minutes with comments and questions.

Sticking to the clock tells your audience you respect their time. Running over (or notably under) tells them you don't.

Planning Consideration Tip: Prepare a key takeaway slide that works whether you're short on time or have extra time—something you can summarize quickly or expand on if time allows.

Space

As far as I know, there's no limit to the number of slides you can include in a deck. But I've definitely clicked through 75 slides for a project update and thought, *Was all of this necessary?*

Space is a constraint even when it doesn't seem like one. Sure, you can add as many slides as you want, but the more you add, the harder it is for your audience to process what matters.

So, before you start designing your deck, ask yourself: What are my audience's expectations regarding the length of the deck? (Are they expecting a one-slide summary or a comprehensive report?) Remember, the purpose of a deck isn't to include everything you know; it's about providing your audience with what they need.

On occasion, you may face space constraints, such as being asked to prepare only one slide for a shared deck or to keep your presentation under 10 slides. These limits often come from collaborators or leadership setting expectations for a larger meeting or presentation. While such constraints can sometimes feel arbitrary, they are still real. If you are in a position to negotiate for more space, you may gain some flexibility. If not, you'll need to be strategic in how you use the space you're given.

Planning Content

Think of content planning as choosing the menu for a dinner party. Now that you know the purpose and guests, it's time to plan what's being served. You don't need all the ingredients; you just need to plan the menu.

At this point, focus on developing a tentative set of ideas. You can begin to explore ideas by revisiting the purpose of the deck or governing question that your slide deck should answer. As you answer the governing question, capture those ideas because they may become the main topics or points for your slide deck.

The process of developing a tentative set of ideas should also be informed by your audience analysis. Ideas can emerge from the answer to this question: What questions are likely to arise in your audience's mind? If you are not sure where to start, steal a page from the journalist's playbook by asking who, what, why, where, when, how, how much, how often.

Identify What Needs to Be Communicated

Give yourself permission to brainstorm freely as you think through two things: your answer to the governing question and the questions your audience is likely to ask. As you do, you'll start to uncover three building blocks for your slide deck:

1. **Topics:** Broad themes or categories you must cover to accomplish your purpose
2. **Key points:** Within each topic, takeaways the audience should remember
3. **Support:** Evidence, data, and examples that could reinforce your key points

Let's explore each of these building blocks in a bit more detail.

Topics: Topics are the major categories your deck must cover to fulfill its purpose. They give your deck structure and help your audience know what to expect. For example, if your deck's goal is to pitch a new initiative, your topics might include the problem, proposed solution, timeline, and resource needs. Early in the process, your goal is simply to name the topics that deserve attention.

Key Points: Within each topic, key points represent the ideas or takeaways you want your audience to remember. These are the core insights that give your message meaning. For example, under the topic of "proposed solution," your key points might address how the solution works, why it's better than other options, and what benefits it delivers. For now, think in terms of rough statements. What does the audience need to know? What action should they consider? You'll refine these later as you shape your slides.

Support: Support brings your key points to life and makes them credible. This includes facts, data, charts, examples, quotations, or short stories that clarify or reinforce your ideas. Continuing the earlier example, you might support the benefits of your proposed solution with pilot test results, a competitor case study, or a customer quote. Strong support makes your message persuasive.

Capture Your Early Thinking

Don't get caught up in sequencing or formatting yet. Start by focusing on what needs to be communicated. Try one or more of the following approaches to plan your deck:

- **A brainstorming document:** Create a list of potential topics, key points, and supporting ideas in a simple text file. This approach gives you space to think broadly and freely without worrying about structure or slide layout. It's especially useful if you like to write as a way of thinking.
- **Sticky notes or a whiteboard:** Write one idea per sticky note or marker phrase. Seeing your content spatially can make it easier to spot gaps.

Starting this way prevents wasted effort, keeps your thinking flexible, and helps you align your content with both your purpose and your audience's needs.

Let's look at a simple planning outline for a presentation on Personal Branding for college students. The mind map shows how we might define the topics and key points.

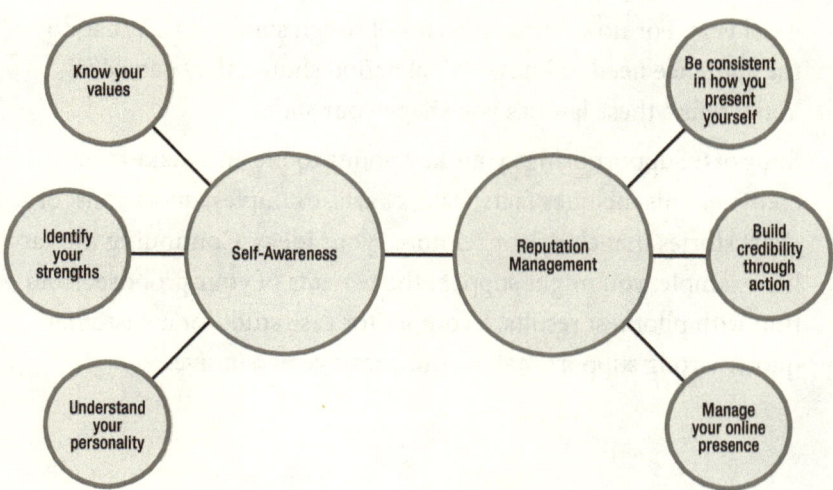

This mind map shows an early-stage content-planning outline with two main topics: Self-Awareness and Reputation Management. Each topic is supported by three key points that reflect what the audience should understand or do. Visual brainstorming tools like this help presenters generate and organize ideas before refining structure or sequencing.

Content planning is messy at first. While the example mind map may appear polished now, it started as a rough list of ideas. Moreover, as you plan your deck and move to the structuring stage, the preliminary content may evolve, and you may later add—or omit—topics, key points, and support.

Although skilled communicators plan their content before preparing their slides, they remain flexible as they draft, because they discover much of what they want to communicate as they compose and revise.

■ ■ ■

Think of planning a slide deck like planning a dinner party. You wouldn't start cooking before deciding why you're hosting the event. (A birthday dinner is different from a formal business gathering.) You'd consider who's coming and their dietary preferences. You'd also put some thought into the kind of experience you'd like them to have. And of course, you'd choose the menu.

Building a presentation works in a similar way:

- Your purpose for communicating is like deciding what kind of dinner party you're hosting.
- Your audience is like your guest list.
- Your audience's preferences are like their dietary needs.
- Your content is like the menu.

Just as a dinner party without planning might leave guests hungry or inundated with mismatched dishes, a slide deck made by someone who hasn't clarified what matters risks confusing the audience, wasting time, or failing to achieve its purpose.

Chapter 2 Takeaways

- Clarify your communication purpose before building your slide deck—whether it's to inform, persuade, update, or engage.

- Define a governing question that keeps your message focused and helps your audience understand the point of the deck.

- Analyze your audience to tailor your message to their needs, knowledge level, attitudes, goals, decision-making styles, and communication preferences.

- Consider practical constraints like how much time you have to prepare or present and how much space your audience expects you to use.

- Avoid assuming your audience thinks like you do. Seek input, ask clarifying questions, and test assumptions early in the planning process.

- Plan your content before designing slides—identifying topics, key points, and supporting evidence that align with your purpose and audience needs.

- Treat planning as a tool, not a chore. Planning helps ensure your message is relevant, focused, and easier to produce and deliver effectively.

In this chapter, you've learned how to define your purpose for communication, analyze your audience, identify constraints, and map out the key content. Now comes the next challenge. How do you structure your message? In chapter 3, you'll learn how to take everything you gathered and shape it into a story that makes sense for your audience.

Map the Structure
of Your Story

Tyler was preparing his first presentation for the state legislative budget subcommittee. As a junior policy analyst, he'd spent weeks collecting data and recommendations on rural broadband expansion. Wanting to be thorough, he built a slide deck with detailed maps, funding models, case studies, and research citations—organized roughly in the order he'd gathered them.

His supervisor skimmed through the draft and frowned. "There's a lot of good information here," she said, "but I'm not sure what story you're telling."

Tyler hadn't thought of it as a story. He thought he was just ... reporting.

That night, he laid out all his content on a whiteboard and started to group related ideas. He realized that his material could be organized around three core questions: *What's the current state? What's the cost of inaction? What's the proposed path forward?* That structure gave his deck a clear arc. It mirrored how the subcommittee would need to think about the issue.

When he presented the revised version, legislators asked thoughtful follow-ups, requested specific data from a key slide, and quoted his conclusions later in session.

Tyler's content didn't change, but the additional planning helped him develop a clear structure for the deck.

———————————◼———————————

Mapping the structure of your story gives your audience a clear path to follow. It helps them understand how your ideas connect and what they should take away.

Just like other forms of communication, slide decks have a macro-structure: a beginning, a middle, and an end. This chapter focuses on the middle—how to arrange your content in a way that serves your audience and supports your purpose for communicating. You'll learn about openings and closings later in the book, in the chapter on special-purpose slides. For now, it's more useful to focus on the middle of the deck—because once the middle is in place, the rest tends to come together more easily.

The ideas from chapter 2, especially the process of mapping out your key points and supporting material, will inform decisions you make when shaping the structure of the middle of your slide deck.

This chapter will help you refine that structure by showing you how to:

- Group your ideas, define your main sections, apply the MeCeFe principles, and sequence your content
- Incorporate story across sections, across slides, and even within a single slide
- Understand why it's important to plan structure before you build slides—and how jumping into software too soon can cost you time and clarity

Establish a Tentative Structure[1]

An effective structure helps your audience grasp the logic of your ideas. Sometimes that structure follows a familiar pattern based on the situation. But even when an established structure is available, don't assume it's the best one for your goals.

In this section of the chapter, you'll learn how to:

1. Look for opportunities to group together similar ideas.
2. Determine the main sections of your deck.
3. Test the tentative structure by applying MeCeFe principles.
4. Sequence the sections for flow.

As you begin planning the structure of your deck, you can continue to capture your ideas on sticky notes, a whiteboard, or in a text document, but resist the urge to define the structure of your deck within presentation software just yet.

Look for Opportunities to Group Together Similar Ideas

This is the time to organize ideas into logical groupings—by identifying similarities among individual items. This step is like making an effective grocery list. Rather than writing a random list of items to purchase, you can make your shopping trip more efficient by grouping similar items: apples and oranges, carrots and spinach, peanut butter and jelly.

Right now, we aren't concerned about the sequence; we simply want to place items into groups.

By looking for patterns among ideas, we make our lives easier when preparing our decks, and our audience appreciates the groupings rather than a long list of ideas.

You may be able to recognize patterns in your ideas by looking for natural categories. Try to identify the common features among the ideas you gathered—an activity that is like sorting ideas into buckets.

For example, if someone asked you to sort an apple, an orange, a lime, broccoli, a carrot, and a red pepper, how would you do it?

One way would be by color:

- **Red bucket:** apple and red pepper
- **Orange bucket:** orange and carrot
- **Green bucket:** lime and broccoli

That makes sense, since our brains naturally look for visual patterns. But another reasonable way to sort the items would be by food type:

- **Fruit bucket:** apple, orange, lime
- **Vegetable bucket:** broccoli, carrot, pepper

The best grouping would depend on the context. A dietitian might group foods by type to talk about balanced meals. But a kindergarten teacher might sort by color for a fun learning activity about healthy foods.

In reality, identifying groupings is likely to be a more complex process than I've presented here.

In Practice

If you are outlining in a text document, every topic, key point, and piece of support may start as a top-level bullet, making them appear equal. But it's best to give your outline shape by organizing ideas according to their role in your message. Main topics stay top-level bullets, key points become second-level bullets, and supporting evidence becomes third-level bullets.

Here's what that structure might look like in a basic outline:

I. Topic A
    a. Key Point 1A
        i. Supporting evidence
        ii. Supporting evidence
    b. Key Point 2A
        i. Supporting evidence
        ii. Supporting evidence
II. Topic B
    a. Key Point 1B
        i. Supporting evidence
        ii. Supporting evidence

b. Key Point 2B
  i. Supporting evidence
  ii. Supporting evidence

This structure helps you visualize the hierarchy of your ideas. In practice, most arguments won't be perfectly balanced. Some topics may have more key points than others, and some points may require more evidence.

Determine the Main Sections

As you sort ideas into groups, you may naturally label the groups. In the earlier example, the groups were labeled Red, Orange, and Green. These labels become the main sections or subsections in your slide deck.

How do you determine the main sections?

If you haven't yet identified your main sections or aren't satisfied with your labels, you can take one of two approaches: a grouping structure or a series-of-questions structure.

1. **Grouping structure:** Label each group with a title that speaks to the similarities among the ideas. Imagine the purpose of the deck is to inform the senior leadership about the feasibility of expanding into new markets. The governing question is, What do we know about the feasibility of expanding into new markets?

   Imagine that you have grouped together the following ideas:

   A. Consumer behavior, industry shifts, emerging competitors

   B. Supply chain, workforce considerations, regulatory issues

   C. Cost projections, revenue potential, investment requirements

The main sections for the deck could be: A. Market Trends, B. Operational Challenges, and C. Financial Considerations.

Instead of labeling the groups by topic, we could use the series-of-questions approach.

2. **Series-of-questions structure:** Sometimes, you can identify the main sections of a slide deck using a series of questions. Imagine

you've already grouped your ideas for a presentation about business expansion. The next step is to ask, What question does each group help answer? Those questions can then serve as the main sections of your deck. Here's what that might look like:

- Consumer behavior, industry shifts, emerging competitors
  - ▸ What trends indicate an opportunity for expansion?
- Supply chain, workforce considerations, regulatory issues
  - ▸ What operational challenges might affect our ability to expand?
- Cost projections, revenue potential, investment requirements
  - ▸ What financial considerations could impact the feasibility of expansion?

How Many Sections Should a Slide Deck Have?

There's no magic number for how many sections your slide deck should have, but two key considerations can help you decide: How few is too few, and how many is too many?

1. **Minimum:** If you are including sections in your deck, you need at least two. Otherwise, you're not really creating sections. The same rule applies for subsections. If you are including subsections within a section, there must be at least two subsections.

   Breaking a deck into too many small sections can feel disjointed. If a section only has one slide, it might not be a section at all. If you find that one section contains only one slide, you should consider grouping related slides into a broader section. For example, if you have a one-slide "challenges" section, consider combining it with the "opportunities" section and renaming the section "Challenges and Opportunities."

2. **Maximum:** While there's no upper limit for the number of sections, research suggests most individuals can't hold more than three or four ideas in their working memory. If you find yourself with too many sections, consider these strategies to create subsections:

A. **Group sections under a bigger category.** Instead of having too many top-level sections, look for themes that naturally group ideas together. This allows you to create a new section while turning the original sections into subsections.

B. **Convert the ideas into subsections.** If you find an idea that may take two or more slides to communicate, the main idea may become a subsection with multiple supporting slides. For example, if each topic (consumer behavior, industry shifts, emerging competitors) includes more than one idea, the ideas could become subsections, and the multiple ideas could map to individual slides.

In Practice: At this point, you should have clear groupings of ideas. Now, name the big categories. These will likely become your deck's main sections. If you struggle to name a section, that might be a sign that your grouping needs more attention.

Test the Tentative Structure by Applying MeCeFe Principles

Within any logically structured slide deck, every set of sections (and sub-sections) should follow three rules. In *The Pyramid Principle*, Barbara Minto introduces two of them explicitly. The ideas in a group should be mutually exclusive (Me) and collectively exhaustive (Ce). That means that each idea in a group should be distinct (no overlap), and together, the ideas should fully cover the topic (no gaps).[2]

Minto also alludes to a third principle—though she doesn't label or emphasize it as directly. She suggests that items grouped together should be of the same kind or serve the same function. My colleague Craig Snow has built on Minto's framework by giving that third principle equal weight: functionally equivalent (Fe).

Together, the three principles—mutually exclusive (Me), collectively exhaustive (Ce), and functionally equivalent (Fe)—offer a way to evaluate the structure of a slide deck. Your sections should be distinct, complete, and parallel.

Here's what that means:

- **Mutually exclusive (Me):** No overlap. Each section should be distinct. If two sections cover similar material, you might need to redefine them or combine them into one.

  Example: If one section is "Customer Retention Strategies" and another is "Loyalty Program Initiatives," ask whether loyalty programs are just a subset of retention strategies. If so, they likely belong in the same section.

- **Collectively exhaustive (Ce):** Nothing missing. Your sections should cover everything your audience expects to see. If you intentionally leave something out, acknowledge it so your audience knows you didn't just forget it.

  Example: If you're presenting an expansion strategy and only discuss market trends and operational challenges, your audience may wonder why financial considerations aren't addressed.

- **Functionally equivalent (Fe):** Keep all items in a set conceptually parallel. Each item should feel like siblings, not a distant relative. That means grouping items that are the same kind of thing—like strategies with strategies, risks with risks, or metrics with metrics.

  Example: If you're presenting key performance indicators and include "Operating Margin" and "Return on Investment," but then add "Expand into new markets," your grouping may feel inconsistent. The first two are financial metrics; the third is a strategic initiative. To keep the set functionally equivalent, group metrics with metrics and strategies with strategies.

  If two or more items are the same kind of thing, but any remaining items are a different kind of thing, the structure is likely to be flawed.

Use these three questions to ensure your main sections are structured effectively:

- Are the sections distinct? (Mutually exclusive)
- Do the sections answer the governing question? (Collectively exhaustive)

- Do the sections feel conceptually parallel?
  (Functionally equivalent)

In Practice: A pyramid diagram can help you map the structure of your story and assess whether your structure satisfies the MeCeFe principles. If your content feels repetitive, incomplete, or jumbled, your sections may need adjusting before moving forward. The diagram here provides a visual way to check whether your ideas are distinct, complete, and conceptually parallel.

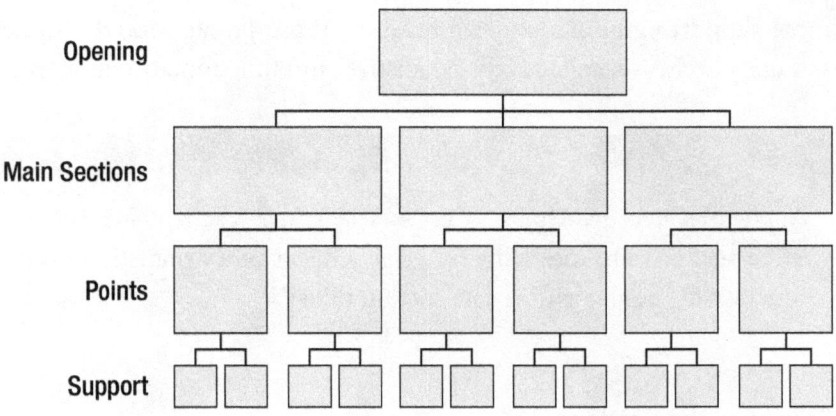

At the top of the pyramid, place the core message: your governing question and the answer. This information represents the opening of your slide deck.

The next layer down includes the main sections of your deck. These sections unpack your main message. Like every layer of the pyramid, these sections should be mutually exclusive, collectively exhaustive, and functionally equivalent.

What happens at the next layer depends on the complexity of your content:

- In shorter or more straightforward decks, the next layer may consist of your main points, each of which often becomes its own slide.

- In longer or more layered decks, the next level might include subsections within each main section. These subsections are then followed by main points, which again may correspond to stand-alone slides.

The bottom layer of the pyramid always includes your supporting information—the content that provides evidence, illustration, or detail.

The MeCeFe principles apply at every horizontal level of the pyramid. That means you should assess not just your main sections but also each set of subsections or supporting points. For example, if one slide has three supporting points under a heading, those points should also be mutually exclusive, collectively exhaustive, and functionally equivalent.

Try This with AI

Apply MeCeFe principles. "Can you help me test whether these three sections are mutually exclusive, collectively exhaustive, and functionally equivalent? [paste section titles]"

Sequence the Sections

Once you have grouped related ideas, labeled the sections, and applied MeCeFe principles, you may have discovered a suitable sequence for the middle of the deck. If not, consider one of the following five ways to sequence or arrange the middle of your slide deck.

In each of the ways to sequence, you are attempting to identify relationships between sections. Some ideas belong together because they're connected logically. For example, some ideas naturally lead to others (causes lead to effects, problems lead to solutions).

1. **By degree:** When you sequence sections by degree, you can choose from a variety of options (or vice versa).
   - Importance: most to least
   - Size: largest to smallest

- Value: most to least recommended
- Ease: easiest to hardest

A business proposal might start with the most important recommendation first. In contrast, a training deck might move from basic ideas (easier) to more advanced concepts (harder) to help audience members build their understanding.

2. **By chronology:** If time plays a key role in your message, consider using a chronological sequence so your audience can see how events unfold over time.
   - Most to least recent
   - Least to most recent
   - Before, during, after

3. **By function:** When different parts of your content serve different roles, function-based sequencing allows your audience to follow along easily.
   - Component parts of a whole
   - Points of agreement, followed by points of disagreement
   - Strength followed by weaknesses
   - Problem-solution

4. **By discovery process:** Some decks work best when they mirror the discovery process, leading the audience through how a conclusion was reached. This sequencing may be appropriate if you need to conform to the norms of a particular group (e.g., an academic conference presentation in which you present the results of empirical research).
   - Problem, method, solution
   - Hypothesis, findings, implications

5. **By audience questions:** When you anticipate that your audience will have specific questions, you can sequence your ideas by the questions they have.

- What's wrong? How do we fix it?
- What to do? Why do it? Where to begin?
- What is it? What does it mean? Why is it important?
- What exactly does it entail? How does it benefit us? What does it cost?
- What is the cause and effect?

The structure you choose shapes the flow of your story and creates a path that guides your audience through your thinking.

What If You Are Uncertain About Which Sequencing Approach to Use?

When in doubt about which sequence to use, you should consider sequencing your content from most important to least important. Research suggests that people are more likely to recall the first (primacy effect) and last (recency effect) pieces of information.[3] If your most important point is in the middle, it's more likely to be missed or forgotten.

Workplace audiences typically want to find the most important information quickly. By leading with what is most relevant to your audience, a technique known in some organizations as the bottom-line-up-front (BLUF) approach, you increase the likelihood that they capture the key point before they stop listening or reading.

An added benefit of using this sequence is that it forces you to prioritize. Sequencing sections in order of importance pushes you to be clear about what really matters to your audience.

How Do You Approach Sequencing Within Sections?

The approach you use as you sequence the main sections may be different than the approach you use as you sequence items within a section.

For example, if your supervisor asked you to look into rising expenses and present cost-savings initiatives, you might sequence your main sections by function, using the problem-recommendation structure. Within the problem section, you might sequence your points by audience questions: What is the problem? What are the causes? What is the significance? Within the recommendation section, you might sequence your points by degree, using the most to least important structure.

How Should You Structure Your Deck If You Don't Have Sections?

Not every deck needs formally labeled sections (especially if it's relatively brief). But that doesn't mean you should skip the thinking process behind grouping and sectioning your content. Before you jump to sequencing, take a moment to test whether natural groupings exist.

Even in a brief deck, you are likely to find clusters of ideas that naturally belong together. Even if you don't label sections, grouping ideas mentally can help you sequence them more effectively. If no clear groups exist, focus on sequencing.

When a deck doesn't have sections, the order of your slides does the heavy lifting. You should use the sequencing approach that makes the most sense for your purpose.

When Does a Deck Move from a Series of Individual Slides to a Set of Sections with Slides?

If any of the following is true, it's time to think in terms of sections rather than just slides:

- The deck extends beyond about 10 slides and is without sections, making it difficult to absorb the flow of ideas.
- There are distinct shifts in topics that need clear separation.
- The audience would benefit from visual signposts to stay oriented.
- The deck is designed for asynchronous reading and needs clear navigation.

If your deck begins to feel like a collection of disconnected slides rather than a cohesive story, consider breaking it into sections—and for longer decks, possibly subsections. Each slide within a section should make a single, focused point that supports that section's main idea.

Tell a Story

One of the most adaptable story structures is the Situation–Complication–Resolution (SCR) framework. It helps you explain the current state, what has disrupted it, and what action or conclusion follows.[4]

This three-part arc can be applied across different levels of a deck:

- **At the macrostructure level,** SCR can shape the full arc of your deck—serving as the basis for three main sections.

- **Within a single section,** SCR can guide how you sequence a handful of related slides.

- **On an individual slide,** SCR can be used to structure the heading, subheading, and body content.

Let's apply this framework to a common business challenge: An external event (like inflation) has increased operational costs.

Macrostructure: Story Across Main Sections

Imagine you're building a deck for senior leadership to evaluate the impact of inflation and consider a response.

- **Section 1 (situation):** Provide an overview of the company's current cost structure and recent financial performance. *Operating costs have remained stable over the past three years, supporting consistent margins.*

- **Section 2 (complication):** Describe the change in external conditions. *Inflation has led to a 12% increase in supplier costs over the last two quarters.*

- **Section 3 (resolution):** Propose how the company could respond. *We recommend three adjustments: renegotiating supplier contracts, adjusting pricing, and targeting internal efficiency gains.*

When you use the SCR framework to guide the macrostructure of your deck, you may need to use multiple slides within each section to elaborate on each part of the framework.

Within a Section: Story Across a Few Slides

Continuing with the inflation example, let's consider how we could apply the SCR framework in the complication section over three slides:

- **Slide A (situation):** Our cost structure has historically been weighted toward raw materials and logistics.
- **Slide B (complication):** Raw material costs have spiked due to inflation and global supply disruptions.
- **Slide C: (resolution):** We've identified three immediate areas for cost containment to offset this pressure.

The resolution slide signals the proposed change and sets up the next section of the deck.

On a Single Slide: Story Within a Slide

Even one slide can tell a mini story using the SCR framework—though not necessarily in that order. In slide design, it's often most effective to lead with the resolution, especially when your audience expects clear recommendations up front. The complication and situation can still appear, but they follow the main point rather than build toward it. Here's an example:

1. **Heading (Resolution):** We recommend renegotiating supplier contracts to manage rising costs.
2. **Subheading (Complication):** Inflation has increased supplier rates by 12%, reducing gross margin.
3. **Slide Body Content (Situation)**
   - Graphic 1: A chart showing supplier costs increasing over time (supporting the complication)
   - Graphic 2: A callout showing potential saving from renegotiation (supporting the resolution)

You don't need to use SCR on every slide, in every section, or across every deck. But knowing how to apply this framework gives you options to tell a compelling story.

Avoid the Pitfalls of Building Too Soon

Structuring your ideas within presentation software can be effective for slide decks with a limited number of key points. We've all done it. You can outline your key points in the notes section and begin building individual slides.

However, for complex decks, jumping to presentation software can make it hard to structure your ideas effectively. While it is easy to drag slides around, a variety of issues can emerge:

- **You lock in section dividers too soon.** If you create section slides before grouping your ideas, you might later realize that two sections should be combined—or that a section should actually be a subsection. Now you may have to go back and redo slides that should never have existed in the first place.

- **You overload content slides.** If you start building individual slides before stepping back to see how much support each key point needs, you risk stuffing too much content onto one slide, forcing extra work later.

- **You structure based on slides rather than ideas.** Presentation software encourages a linear approach, making it harder to spot structural gaps, redundancies, or opportunities to group ideas logically.

- **You lose flexibility.** Once slides are created, you may resist moving ideas around or cutting content, simply because you've spent time producing it—even when doing so would make the deck better.

Chapter 3 Takeaways

- Structure shapes meaning by providing a clear, intentional flow that helps your audience follow and retain your message.

- Start by grouping similar ideas before worrying about sequence. Clustering content reveals patterns and creates the foundation for a logical structure.

- Label your groups to form main sections, using either topic-based or question-based headings, depending on what best supports your purpose and audience.

- Test your structure using MeCeFe principles to ensure sections are mutually exclusive, collectively exhaustive, and functionally equivalent.

- Sequence your sections strategically using common patterns like importance, chronology, function, discovery process, or audience questions.

- Use sectioning when your deck is long or when your audience would benefit from clear visual signposts and topic shifts.

- Consider using the Situation-Complication-Resolution (SCR) framework to introduce narrative logic across your deck, within a section, or even on a single slide.

- Plan your structure before building slides, to increase clarity, prevent waste, and reduce rework later.

Once you've mapped out the structure of your deck, there's one more critical question to consider in the planning stage: How much information should go on each slide? That's the focus of the next chapter. You'll learn how to gauge the right level of detail, avoid overloading your audience, and make smart choices about how much information to include.

Consider the Information Density of Your Deck

When Sloan joined a well-respected consulting firm right out of graduate school, she brought with her a carefully honed design instinct: Keep it simple, keep it clean. Her business school professors had drilled the point home—slides should be visual, minimalist, and easy to absorb at a glance.

Three months into the job, Sloan was asked to prepare a slide deck for one of the firm's top clients, a deck that summarized the research she had completed during the first six weeks of the engagement. The audience, a senior VP from the client's firm, would receive the slides in advance, use them to guide a conversation with their team, and later circulate the deck internally to colleagues who would not be present at the meeting.

It was clear: This deck wasn't just a presentation aid. It *was* the deliverable.

Sloan started drafting the opening slides with the clean style she had learned in school. But when she looked through the firm's archive for examples, her confidence wavered. The decks she found were dense. Text and visuals filled nearly every inch of space. Headings were descriptive, charts were complex, and annotations were everywhere. These weren't slides anyone could glance at and easily absorb. They were documents written for close reading—prepared for teams who expected detail and depth.

Now she wasn't sure what to do. If she followed what she was taught, would her slides seem too light? But if she matched what she saw around her, would she end up overloading the audience?

She opened a blank slide, took a breath, and started thinking not just about what to include but how much.

Slide deck design is as varied as the context in which it's used. While much of the guidance around creating slides encourages simplicity and minimalism, the reality of professional communication often demands something more. Most guidance tends to focus on low-density slides but offers limited details for crafting effective decks that handle complex information and challenging communication situations. In this chapter, we'll explore how to determine the right level of information density for your deck.

The quantity of information in a slide deck impacts how an audience processes, retains, and acts on it. Before you begin producing slides, you should consider the information density of the set of slides you plan to create.

What Is Information Density?

Information density reflects the amount of content—text and graphic elements—included on a slide. It's a choice you make about how much information is necessary to communicate your point effectively.

You may be unfamiliar with the term *information density*, but I've found it to be a straightforward concept that audiences easily grasp and quickly incorporate into their own discussions about slide decks.

You can understand information density by focusing on two features: word count and information chunks.

- **Word count** refers to the total number of words on a slide. This includes headings, body text, labels in graphics, and any text within charts and tables (numerals like 80,000 count as a single word). Word count does not include footnotes.

- **Information chunk** refers to any content your audience perceives as belonging to a distinct group, separate from other groups around it.[1] Chunks can take many forms—a bulleted list, a paragraph of text, a chart, an image with a caption, or a combination of these elements.

As word count and information chunks increase, so does the cognitive effort required from your audience to understand your message.

How Can You Apply Information Density When Planning Your Deck?

Information density exists on a spectrum ranging from slides with minimal content to those with detailed information. This continuum reflects the countless ways slides can be designed to convey a message. However, for clarity, we'll explore information density through three broad categories: low, medium, and high density.[2] To help you plan the overall density of your deck, the following table offers a basic framework that maps word count and information chunks to three density levels.

A Framework for Choosing Slide Density

Density Level	Word Count	Information Chunks
Low	Low	Low
Medium	Medium	Medium
High	High	High

This framework provides a broad way to think about information density. While this chapter focuses on planning the overall level of density across your slide deck, chapter 7 explains how to manage it on individual slides.

To see how these density levels translate into design choices, let's look at three versions of the same slide. Each version uses the same heading and graphic but differs in the amount of supporting text and the number of distinct information chunks.[3] The examples move from low to high density.

The first version shows a minimal approach with only a single graphic and very little text.

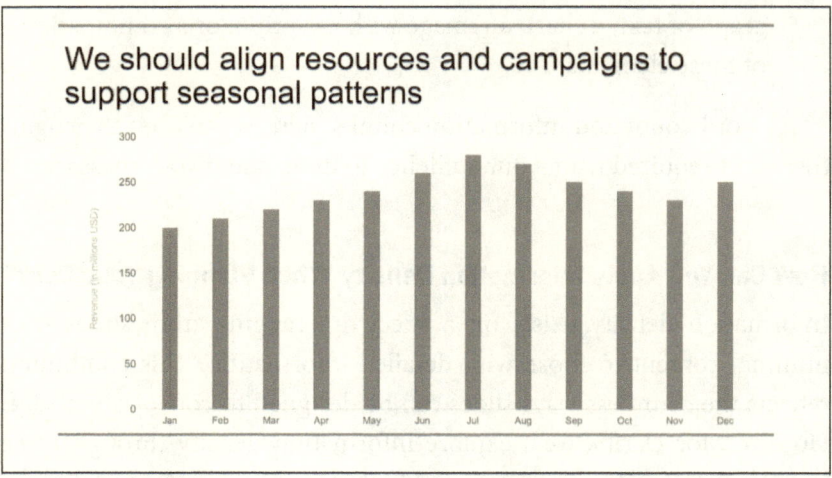

This low-word-count slide with one information chunk contains a single chart and a heading, providing a clear takeaway without additional explanation. This slide is ideal for live presentation settings where the speaker will elaborate on the point verbally.

The second version adds moderate textual support to the same graphic.

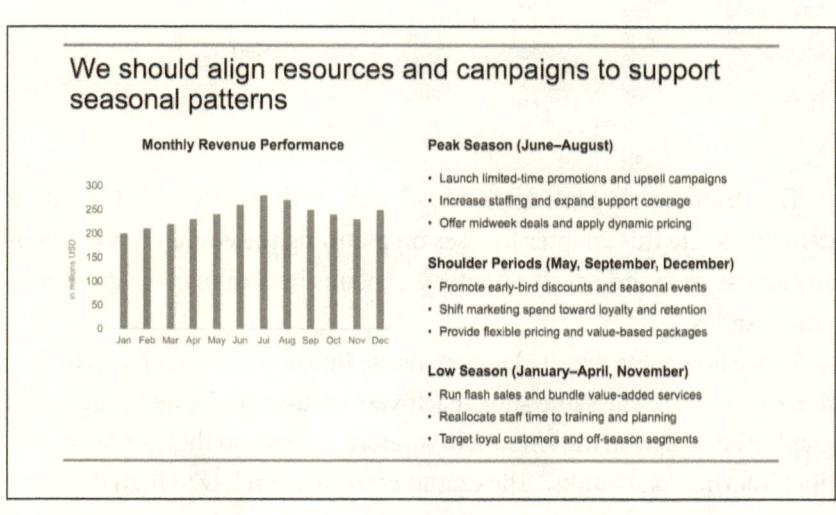

This is a medium-word-count slide with two information chunks that includes bullet points alongside the chart. The extra details support audience comprehension without creating unnecessary cognitive load, making it appropriate for team updates or discussion-driven meetings.

The third version includes one graphic and detailed written support.

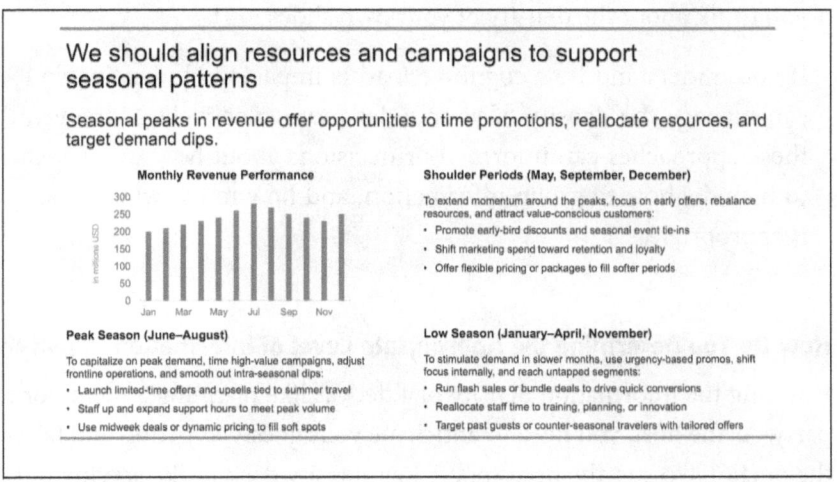

This high-word-count slide with four information chunks includes a chart paired with detailed recommendations for three seasonal periods. The result is a self-contained slide, well suited for asynchronous review, executive briefings, or leave-behinds.

Measuring Information Density

Researchers from a variety of academic fields have taken the following approaches to measure the information density of slides:

- **Content-to-space ratio:** Calculate the proportion or percentage (25%, 50%, 75%, 100%) of a slide occupied by content.
- **White space:** Calculate the percentage of a slide left blank.
- **Word count:** Count the number of words on a slide.
- **Paragraph count:** Count the number of paragraphs on a slide.

- **Element count:** Count number of visual elements on the slide.
- **Proportion of graphic content**: Estimated from none, ⅛, ¼, ⅓, or the whole.

While these academic methods offer precision, you are unlikely to apply them directly. Nevertheless, these approaches can shape how you think about the density of your own slides.

If you understand how cognitive load is impacted by density, you can manage the density of your slides more effectively. Moreover, these approaches can inform your decisions about how much text to include, how to group information, and how much white space is appropriate.

How Do You Determine the Appropriate Level of Information Density?

Planning the information density of a deck is like planning a menu for a party. As the host, you need to anticipate your guests' appetites and tailor the portions to suit the occasion. A low-density deck is like serving hors d'oeuvres—small, simple portions that are easy to consume. A medium-density deck is like preparing a well-balanced meal—satisfying but not too heavy, ideal for most occasions. A high-density deck is akin to hosting a banquet—a feast of detail that requires time and focus to fully appreciate.

Just as a thoughtful host adjusts the menu to the occasion, you should tailor the information density of your slide deck based on its function and audience's expectations. To guide your decision, start by asking two questions:

- Will this deck be presented live, read asynchronously, or both?
  - ▸ **Live presentation:** Aim for a low-density deck to let your spoken words do the work.
  - ▸ **Asynchronous reading:** Aim for high-density deck to ensure ideas are self-contained.
  - ▸ **Both:** Aim for a medium-density deck that balances clarity and flexibility.

- What level of detail does my audience expect?
  - **Big-picture insights only:** Keep slides low density.
  - **Some context and analysis:** Consider medium density.
  - **Thorough explanations and evidence:** Choose high density.

To help you apply these questions, the table summarizes how presentation context and audience expectations often align with different levels of information density.

Match Context and Audience Needs to Information Density

Context	How the Deck Will Be Used	What the Audience Needs	Recommended Density
Presenting live	A visual aid for an in-person or virtual presentation	Big-picture insights with speaker-driven explanation	Low
Guiding a discussion	A hybrid document that helps focus the conversation	A mix of takeaways and supporting details	Medium
Reading independently	A stand-alone document for asynchronous consumption	Self-contained detail without the need for spoken content	High

Even with these recommendations, you will find that choosing the right level of information density involves judgment. Two additional steps can help:

- **Ask your audience or stakeholders what they find most useful.** You don't need to use the word *density*—you can ask whether they prefer big-picture insights, a deck that can stand alone, or something in between.

- **Review past decks used in similar situations.** Look at the level of detail included and ask: Did it help achieve the communication objective? Was it too sparse or too dense to be effective?

Remember, just because a certain level of density was used before doesn't mean it was the right choice—or that your audience will want the same thing now.

To help you make informed choices about information density, let's take a closer look at each level of information density on its own. When is it most effective? What are its advantages? What challenges does it introduce? By understanding these nuances, you will be able to make choices that align with your audience's expectations. In addition, by considering the information density of a slide deck during the planning stages, you will reduce the need for significant redesign later, saving time and effort.

Low-Density Slide Decks

Low-density slides have minimal content (i.e., fewer words and fewer information chunks). A low-density set of slides is best suited to accompany a speaker and support the points conveyed orally. This approach meets the needs of audiences who only require a high level of information or the big picture. Low-density decks are appropriate in a variety of situations where the deck's primary role is to support—not replace—the speaker:

- **Executive briefings:** Situations where you need to present a high-level update to senior leaders
- **Leadership talks:** Slides aimed to support a presentation that communicates a vision or strategy
- **Client or prospect meeting:** Situations where the focus is on building relationships
- **Ballroom-type presentations** (e.g., keynote, TED-style talk): Audiences expect big-picture insights rather than dense information

To weigh the benefits and trade-offs of low-density decks, review the advantages and challenges summarized in the next table.

Advantages and Challenges of Low-Density Decks

Advantages	Challenges
Faster to produce: With fewer visual elements, low-density slides require less time to design.	**Risk of oversimplification:** Important context or supporting details may be left out.
Flexibility: With less information, the speaker can adapt the message for various audiences.	**Dependence on verbal delivery:** Requires a presenter to fill in the gaps.
Simplicity: Slides with less information are easier to remember.	**Perceived lack of substance:** May appear insufficient to audiences who want details.
	Audience expectations: If the audience expects detailed analysis, low-density slides may make the communicator seem unprepared.

Low-density decks are best used when the audience does not require seeing the slides before a live presentation or have the need to reference them afterward.

Medium-Density Slide Decks

Medium-density slides balance graphics, text, and white space. These decks are especially useful when your goal is to guide a discussion between you and the audience. Medium-density slides allow you to provide enough details without crowding the slide. This approach often works well in situations where your audience needs more than a heading, but they don't need every detail spelled out:

- **Team presentations:** Slides that offer enough information to support dialogue and decision-making
- **Workshops:** Slides that depict processes or concepts with a mix of graphic and textual support
- **Progress reports:** Slides that include key takeaways and offer some details
- **Investor decks:** Slides that provide enough evidence to build confidence without bogging down the pitch

The following table summarizes why medium-density decks are often an optimal choice—and what to watch out for when using this approach.

Advantages and Challenges of Medium-Density Decks

Advantages	Challenges
Flexibility across contexts: Medium-density slide decks allow audiences to appropriately digest graphics and text during a live presentation, and they include sufficient details so that the deck can be useful prior to, after, or in place of attending the live presentation.	**Risk of mediocrity:** If not designed well, medium-density decks can feel unremarkable.
Clarity with substance: The deck contains just enough depth to be useful without slowing down comprehension.	**Balancing act:** Finding the right level of detail can be tricky.

Medium-density decks are like the Swiss Army knife of decks—they provide a versatile middle ground and are well suited for a wide range of presentation contexts.

High-Density Slide Decks

A high-density slide deck provides comprehensive content that stands on its own. They are especially useful when your audience needs to absorb information independently—either because you won't be there to present or because the situation requires detailed documentation.

High-density slide decks are best suited for situations that call for detail, depth, and self-sufficiency:

- **Technical presentations:** Situations requiring detailed evidence such as financial analysis, scientific findings, or project plans
- **Reference materials:** Slide decks that will be used post-presentation for detailed study or decision–making
- **Compliance or audit reports:** Situations where formal documentation is required
- **Client deliverables:** Decks intended to convey detailed recommendations, research, or results

The following table captures the key strengths of high-density decks, as well as the potential drawbacks you'll need to manage.

Advantages and Challenges of High-Density Decks

Advantages	Challenges
Completeness: Ensure all relevant details are included, reducing the need for a live presenter.	**Cognitive overload:** High-density decks can exceed what audiences can process in real time.
Utility: Add long-term value by doubling as handouts or reference guides.	**Reduced clarity:** Without careful design, high-density decks may appear cluttered and difficult to read.

High-density decks are valuable when your audience expects detailed content they can review independently. But to avoid overloading your readers, you'll need to pair that depth with thoughtful organization, visual clarity, and a sharp understanding of what your audience truly needs.

That said, high-density slides still show up in live presentation settings—not because they're ideal, but because they've become routine in many workplaces. While I don't recommend using dense slides as visual aids during a talk, I've seen it happen enough to know it's not going away. Rather than pretend the practice doesn't exist, let's take a practical approach: How can you reduce friction for your audience when high-density decks are the norm?

In the next section, we'll tackle some of the common questions that come up when balancing competing demands around information density:

- Can a single slide deck include content slides with varying levels of information density?
- Should you prepare one slide deck for presenting and another for distribution?
- What do you do when a single deck needs to serve multiple functions?
- What level of density is best when presenting online?

Most of these questions don't have one-size-fits-all answers, but there are sound strategies that can help you make smart, audience-centered choices.

Can a Single Slide Deck Include Content Slides with Varying Levels of Information Density?

Yes. While it's important to maintain a consistent look and feel, your top priority should be supporting your communication goal. That means it's perfectly acceptable to vary the information density across slides when it helps your audience. For example, if most of your deck uses medium-density slides, don't force extra content onto a low-density slide. And if one key slide needs to be high-density to be useful, don't hold it back just to match the rest. Let function—not uniformity—guide your decisions.

The examples below show how different combinations of density levels can work well in practice.

- **Low-density deck with medium- or high-density slides:**
  A sales pitch may use low-density slides for visual impact; however, medium- or high-density slides may be included to address specific concerns or detailed pricing information.

- **Medium-density deck with low- and high-density slides:**
  A client presentation may rely on medium-density slides to tell the story, while occasional low-density slides can create impactful moments, and occasional high-density slides can emphasize detailed research.

- **High-density deck with low-density slides:** An investor report may consist of high-density slides that include data and analysis, but low-density slides can be strategically used to highlight key initiatives or point to areas of strategic interest.

Plan your deck with a primary density level in mind, but don't shy away from using a mix of density levels.

Is It Best to Create a Low-Density Deck for a Live Presentation and a Second High-Density Deck to Be Distributed After a Presentation?

Most professionals use a single deck for both situations simply because they don't have time to create two. However, if time isn't a constraint, creating separate decks allows you to tailor each for its unique purpose.

If you decide to create two—a high-density and a low-density version—it's generally best to start with the high-density deck. This approach gives you space to think deeply about your content and reduces the likelihood that you will omit important details. In practice, it's much easier to simplify a high-density deck than to add details to one that's low-density.

What Do You Do When a Deck Needs to Be Suitable in Multiple Contexts?

Create a medium-density deck. When your slide deck needs to work both as a visual aid during a live presentation and as a stand-alone resource afterward, medium density offers the best compromise. This approach provides sufficient detail to support spoken delivery without overloading your audience and enough detail for someone reading on their own.[4]

Your aim should be to produce a deck that complements what you say during the presentation while standing on its own afterward. You want to avoid reading from your slides or asking your audience to choose between listening to you and reading ahead—most people can't really do both. A well-designed medium-density deck makes it easier for listeners to follow your message in real time and for readers to absorb it later without feeling like they've missed something essential.

A medium-density approach may seem simple, but in practice, many presenters struggle to get the balance right. That's because it requires meeting two different audience needs at once: clarity in the room and completeness on the slide. Many presenters have been told to "keep slides simple," but that advice doesn't always apply when your deck must also stand on its own. The dual function creates a natural tension. How can you design a slide that's both simple enough for live delivery and detailed enough for later review?

For some communicators, the challenge is resisting the urge to simplify too much—especially if they've spent years assuming that "good slides" should be as minimalistic as possible. These individuals might hesitate to add the extra clarity needed for readers who aren't in the room. But for many others, the opposite is true. They are already creating slides that are too dense. When these presenters hear that a medium-density deck is the best hybrid approach, they may assume they're already doing it, when in reality, they are still filling their slides with more information than their audience can reasonably process.

Striking the right balance may require deliberate trade-offs and a recognition that your organization's standard practice could still lean too dense. But by planning for both live and post-presentation needs up front, you reduce the need for heavy revision later.

What Level of Density Is Best When Presenting Online?

Medium-density slides often work well for virtual presentations. When people join a Zoom or Teams meeting, they're typically seated close to their screens and viewing on individual monitors. This setup makes it easier for your audience to read text and process visuals compared to in-person settings, where participants may be seated far from a shared screen.

When people attend online meetings from their desks, medium-density slides offer an effective middle ground. In meetings where the goal is to explain, discuss, or make decisions based on the information being presented, sufficient supporting details are helpful.

■ ■ ■

The intended information density of your deck is a critical consideration in the planning process, but before you start producing slides, there's one last tool that can help: storyboarding.

Storyboarding allows you to map out your presentation flow and generate a rough sketch of your content slides before you open your presentation software. As we move into the next section on producing slides, consider how storyboarding can help you make intentional design choices from the start. If you'd like to learn more about storyboarding, visit SlideDeckBook.com to download a brief guide.

Chapter 4 Takeaways

- Information density affects how your audience processes, retains, and responds to your message. Deciding on the information density of your deck is a key planning decision.
- Density is a design choice. Low-density slides aren't automatically better, and high-density slides aren't automatically worse. What matters is alignment with your purpose, audience, and context.
- Information density includes both word count and information chunks. A slide with few words can still feel dense if too many ideas are packed together.
- Your deck's function should guide its density.
  - ▶ Use low-density decks to support live presentations where the speaker provides the detail.

- ▸ Use medium-density decks to guide conversations and provide enough depth for follow-up.
- ▸ Use high-density decks when the slides must stand on their own and communicate complete ideas.
- A single deck can mix levels of density. Adjust the density slide by slide to support your goals—not for the sake of consistency, but for clarity and usefulness.
- Start by planning your primary density level, then adjust with purpose. A clearly defined density plan reduces the need for major redesign later.
- When in doubt, ask or investigate. Talk to your audience or look at past decks to understand expectations, but don't assume that what was done before was ideal.
- If your deck needs to serve multiple purposes, aim for medium density. Medium-density decks offer the best chance of balancing live delivery with post-presentation review.

Choosing the density helps you decide how much information to include on a slide. Now, we move on to building your slides, and we begin by learning to surface your main points at the top of each content slide.

PRODUCING YOUR SLIDE DECKS

Now that you've completed the planning stages for your deck, you are ready to begin producing your slides. This is where your ideas take visual form—where structure turns into story, and key points begin to come to life.

Slide decks are made up of two types of slides. Regardless of the information density of the deck you are creating, your deck will include content slides and special-purpose slides:

- **Content slides**: These carry the substance of your message: the key points, along with corresponding graphic elements and explanatory text.

- **Special-purpose slides**: These guide your audience through the deck's structure. They serve as navigational aids, setting the stage for the deck, summarizing key points, or delineating major sections.

In this part of the book, we'll focus on producing individual content slides. You can begin with content slides or special-purpose slides—or you can move between them as you work. (Special-purpose slides are covered in chapter 8.)

Each chapter in this section addresses a specific step in producing effective content slides:

- **Chapter 5: Clarify the Core Message of the Story**—Learn how to surface your main point and express it clearly through your slide heading.

- **Chapter 6: Determine Supporting Information**—Explore options for using graphic and textual elements to support your message.

- **Chapter 7: Organize Supporting Information**—Discover how to group, arrange, and lay out your content so it's clear and easy for your audience to follow.

This is the part of the book that will help you turn good thinking into great communication.

Clarify the Core Message of the Story

Terri had just joined the strategy team at a multinational food-and-beverage company when her manager asked her to update a slide deck for an upcoming regional strategy review. The audience: the president of the North American business unit, who'd be using the slides to brief other executives and guide a decision-making session the following week.

Terri scanned through the slides and paused at one labeled *"Consumer Segmentation."* It included a heatmap, two pie charts, and a short quote from a focus group. The data was recent and easy to read, but the title left her unsure what the slide was actually saying.

She turned to her manager. "What's the main idea here?"

Her manager shrugged. "It's just the segmentation data. Make sure the visuals are on-brand, and double-check the numbers."

"But what do we want the president to take away from this? That one segment is underperforming? That we're misaligned on targeting?"

Her manager didn't answer directly. "Just match the style from the last deck."

A few days later, during the internal review, the VP of strategy flipped to the same slide and frowned. "I see the data," he said, "but what does it mean?"

No one had a clear answer.

If a slide doesn't clearly surface its main point, even experienced professionals may be left guessing. That's why one of the most important choices you can make is what you include in the heading.

This chapter focuses on how to surface the main point on each content slide—whether you're presenting it live or sharing it as a standalone deliverable. You'll learn the different types of headings, when and how to use each one, and strategies for writing clear headings that guide your audience through your story.

Case Study: What's the Main Point?

Quickly review this example content slide and think about what point you believe the creator of this slide was trying to make.

Customer Channel Preferences		
Channel	**Segment A**	**Segment B**
In-Store	60%	25%
Mobile App	15%	35%
Desktop Site	20%	30%
Phone	5%	10%

When I share this example slide during live training sessions, I ask participants to share the point they think the author of the slide was trying to make. In every instance, participants share a wide variety of points:

- Segment A prefers in-store shopping, while Segment B prefers digital channels.
- Mobile and desktop channels are significantly more important for Segment B than Segment A.
- A one-size-fits-all channel strategy won't work—each segment needs a tailored approach.
- The in-store channel is still dominant for Segment A but much less so for Segment B.
- Phone is the least-preferred channel for both segments.
- Segment B is more digitally engaged than Segment A.
- Segment A shows a strong preference for traditional channels.
- Online channels (mobile + desktop) account for a majority of Segment B's preferences.
- There's a need to improve the mobile experience for Segment A if usage is to increase.
- Marketing resources should be allocated differently by segment.
- Segment B may be younger or more tech-savvy based on their digital preferences.
- In-store investment may yield higher ROI with Segment A.
- There's an opportunity to boost digital adoption in Segment A.
- Channel preference could inform staffing, promotion, or user experience priorities.

If a single slide invites this many interpretations, we can conclude that it's ineffective.

Write the Point Where People Look First

The heading of the slide, conventionally located in the upper-left corner of the slide, is where audience members and readers look first. It's also when communication can begin effectively or begin to break down.

Eye-tracking studies of websites and documents show that readers tend to follow an F-shaped viewing pattern. They begin in the top-left, scan across the top, then backtrack to the left margin and scan downward. The behavior appears to hold for slide decks as well.

In the pages ahead, we'll walk through four key steps for crafting effective slide headings:

1. **Choose the type of heading.** Learn the three types of headings—topic, question, and message—and when to use each one.

2. **Write the heading.** Discover helpful strategies for writing headings that are clear, purposeful, and audience centered.

3. **Decide whether to add a sub-headline.** Explore when a sub-headline can help strengthen your main point or guide your audience through complex information.

4. **Consider using trackers.** Understand how trackers (such as section labels or mini-titles) can help orient your audience in longer decks.

By the end of this chapter, you'll know how to craft headings that communicate your key points directly, help your audience stay focused, and tell a story across your entire deck.

Choose the Type of Heading

You can write a slide heading in one of three ways: topic, question, or message.

Topic Headings

A *topic heading* introduces the subject of a slide without making a specific claim or drawing a conclusion. These headings are useful when your goal is to quickly orient the audience to the content or present information in a neutral way. Topic headings signal what the slide is about, but not what the audience should take away.

To help you use topic headings more intentionally, the tables here outline three key dimensions: type, purpose, and style.

The first table describes three common types of topic headings based on what they introduce.

Types of Topic Headings

Type	Description	Example Heading
Concept-oriented	Introduces an idea	Fundamentals of Building Client Relationships
Process-oriented	Introduces a series of steps	Steps to Strengthening Client Relationships
Data-oriented	Introduces quantitative or qualitative information	Client Satisfaction Trends

Just as you learned in chapter 2 about aligning your communication with your purpose, topic headings can also reflect different goals on a slide. The next table outlines three common purposes.

Purpose of Topic Headings

Purpose	Description	Example Heading
Informational	Introduces a topic in a neutral manner	An Overview of Client Relationship Management Strategies
Instructional	Presents a set of actions for completing a task or achieving a goal	Best Practices for Building Stronger Client Loyalty
Explanatory	Introduces content that explains how something works	Factors Influencing Client Retention

Topic headings can also vary in style. The following table shows how heading style can range from formal to informal.

Styles of Topic Headings

Style	Description	Example Heading
Formal	Uses a professional tone using precise language	Enhancing Client Loyalty through Value Creation
Informal	Uses a conversational tone and simplified language	Ways to Keep Your Clients Coming Back

Topic headings are appropriate when your goal is to introduce content without interpreting it. Keep in mind that if your audience needs to quickly grasp the takeaway, a topic heading may not be enough on its own.

Question Headings

Question headings frame the slide content as an inquiry. They're particularly effective for prompting curiosity, inviting interaction, or guiding the audience through ideas.

The next table outlines four ways question headings can function.

Functions of Question Headings

Function	Example Heading
Focuses attention by directing the audience's attention to a specific issue or concept	What drives guest satisfaction?
Encourages engagement by posing a question the audience wants answered	How will your bonus be calculated?
Frames the discussion	Why do guest satisfaction scores matter?
Organizes the content	What are the steps to an effective customer interaction?

Use question headings when you want to create a sense of inquiry or when your slide is part of a discussion that builds toward a conclusion. They can be especially useful when facilitating dialogue or inviting reflection.

Message Headings

A *message heading* conveys a specific message or key takeaway for the slide. While the idea is widely used, the terminology varies. Consulting firms such as McKinsey, Boston Consulting Group, and Ernst & Young refer to them as *action titles*. Blackstone uses the term *callouts*. Bruce Gabrille prefers *conclusion titles,* while Mary Munter and Lynn Russell use *message titles*. Traci Nathans-Kelly and Christine Nicometo recommend *sentence headers* and Michael Alley and Kathryn Neeley call them *sentence headlines*.[1]

As Cliff Atkinson puts it, slide titles should function like journalistic headlines to help your audience grasp each point quickly.[2] Gene Zelazny adds, "You want a message that's like a newspaper headline—a statement that captures your interest and makes you want to read more."[3]

Placing your main point at the top of the slide follows a bottom-line-up-front-approach to content slide communication. Throughout this book, I'll refer to these message headings as **headlines**.

Headlines can vary in both type and purpose. Even though all are declarative statements, they frame the slide's content in distinct ways. The next table introduces three common types of headlines and how they function.

Headline Types

Headline Type	Description	Example Heading
Insight-oriented	Highlights a meaningful connection or pattern in the data	Employees who feel heard are more likely to stay with their organization
Conclusion-oriented	States the main takeaway or outcomes based on data or analysis presenting	Regular manager-employee check-ins reduce turnover
Recommendation-oriented	Suggests a specific action the audience should take based on the slide's content	Implement monthly one-on-one meetings between managers and direct reports

Use an insight-oriented headline to frame an issue, a conclusion-oriented headline to communicate a result, and a recommendation-oriented headline to suggest a course of action. These headline types work together across a deck to help your audience understand what the information means and what to do with it.

Regardless of which type you choose, your headline should include a strong verb—words like *increase*, *adopt*, or *grow*. Use a headline when your audience expects or wants you to convey the main point, conclusion, or takeaway up front.

Unlike topic headings or question headings, headlines surface the governing thought of the slide: the main point. Headlines benefit readers in three ways:

- By enabling readers to quickly understand the most important information on each slide

- By reducing the risk that readers misinterpret the main point that you are trying to convey

- By meeting the needs of an audience who does not have the time or interest to read the entire slide

Communication scholar Mary Munter refers to these benefits as *skim value*—the idea that audiences should be able to quickly grasp the key message, even when scanning.[4] Research suggests that headlines improve audience comprehension and retention.[5]

Headlines can also be helpful when you are creating a slide deck collaboratively. For example, in many organizations, junior team members create slides that their managers later present. When those slides use only topic titles, the manager—often juggling multiple projects—may not deliver the intended takeaway. A clear headline helps increase the likelihood the main point is clear, even when someone else is presenting the slide.

Many analysts who use headlines also report that they receive better feedback as they collaborate with their managers when creating decks. Clear headlines prompt earlier conversations about the key points and how to support them. These discussions help managers present with greater confidence, and the message is more likely to be better understood by the audience.

Regardless of your workplace role, you might be asked to create a slide (or series of slides) that someone else will present. When you prepare content slides with topic headings, you risk increasing the variation in how the slide will be presented by the speaker and how the message will be interpreted by the audience.

Don't Make Your Audience Guess

You might feel that you don't need to include the point at the top of your slide if you're presenting it to a live audience, but if your slide is going to be shared with an audience before or after your presentation, a headline is essential for clear communication.

You may feel that your point is clear or that your audience could only interpret the slide in only one way, but remember that you may suffer from the curse of knowledge.

Even when a headline is the most appropriate option, why do some communicators still phrase their heading as something other than a point? I have a few thoughts:

1. **They simply don't know the best practice**. These individuals may have never been taught the best way to communicate using a slide deck.

2. **They don't know what their main point is**. If these individuals have not put in the time to clarify their own thinking, they may not know the main idea they want to communicate.

3. **They are reluctant to share their main point**. These individuals may be operating under the misguided assumption that their audience prefers to come to the conclusion on their own.

Instead, in most situations, consider operating under the assumption that your audience prefers to see the main idea up front by placing it at the top of each content slide.

Write the Heading

Whether you're using a topic heading, a question heading, or a headline on your slide, your heading frames the message. You don't need to rigidly follow the guidelines below, but you should aim for consistency across your deck.

- **Limit each heading to no more than two lines.** Avoid leaving one word alone on the second line of a two-line heading. The number of lines in a headline on one slide has no bearing on the number of lines in a headline on the other slides.

- **Use sentence case.** Capitalize only the first letter of the first word and any proper nouns.

- **Align left**. Left-align headings rather than center because the upper-left portion of the slide is where audiences look first.

- **Avoid formatting effects**. Skip all-caps, boldface, italics, and underlining.

- **Use punctuation intentionally**. Include conventional internal punctuation (e.g., commas), but omit end punctuation—except for question headings, which should end with a question mark.

- **Write a complete thought**. For headlines, write a grammatically complete sentence that expresses the main point. (Topic headings don't need to be complete sentences.)

While these guidelines apply broadly to headings, the next section of this chapter focuses on headlines. Headlines are the most effective way to clarify the point for your audience. In this section, you'll learn how to:

- Convert topic headings to headlines
- Use ellipses to link headlines across slides
- Present headlines effectively in a live setting
- Decide when a headline may not be necessary

Convert Topic Headings to Headlines

The question audiences typically ask when looking at a content slide with a topic heading is "What about [insert topic]?" Try it for yourself by reviewing each topic heading in the following table and asking the same question of each one. Then read the headline and consider whether you would have preferred if the slide included the headline listed after each topic heading instead.

Topic Headings to Headlines

Topic Heading	Headline
Assets Under Management	Our assets under management have quadrupled in the last five years
Strategic Advantage	We use proprietary models to confirm the adequacy of cash flows
Philosophy	Investment decisions are based on long-term considerations
Team	Our team has over 100 years of industry experience

As this table shows, converting topic headings to headlines helps clarify the point of each slide. Instead of prompting questions, a well-written headline answers the most important one: "What's the takeaway?"

You may also find that some of the headings you've brainstormed used question headings. If the answer to the question is important, you should consider converting the question into a headline. For example, instead of "Are our retention efforts working?" use "Retention has improved 20% since launching the program."

Try This with AI

Use AI to refine slide headings. *Prompt:* "Here are ten slide headings. Which ones are too vague or generic, and how could I improve them?"

Consider Using Ellipses to Connect Ideas Across Slides

Ellipses indicate there's more to come, building anticipation for the next slide. By using ellipses at the end of one headline, you can continue the thought to the next slide headline. This approach can help you create a sense of continuity and flow across slides. When you use ellipses in slide-deck headlines, you should follow three guidelines:

- Use them sparingly to maintain their impact.
- Ensure they're being used to support the overall flow of the presentation.
- Follow proper punctuation rules (three dots for ellipsis).

When used well, ellipses create a story thread that maintains narrative momentum from slide to slide. Dave McKinsey, author of the book *Strategic Storytelling*, says, "The use of ellipses (…) at the end of one slide title and the beginning of the next is a technique usually reserved for instances where the second slide answers a question triggered by the first."[6] In these cases, ellipses signal a progression from one idea to the next.

When you're creating a deck that will be read rather than presented, using ellipses to connect ideas across slides can be especially effective. Think about how you typically read a deck that's sent as an attachment to an email message. Chances are you open the attachment as a PDF, then

1. Read a headline
2. Briefly scan the visual evidence on the slide
3. Scroll to the next slide
4. Read the next headline
5. And continue ...

Deliver Slides with Headlines Effectively

If you are not used to creating slides with headlines, you may wonder what to say aloud when you display a slide that contains the main message atop the slide. The best presenters know that audiences don't like being read to. However, your audience will likely be forgiving if you only read one clear statement from each slide. Instead of reading aloud the headline word for word, you may consider another approach: Introduce the slide's main idea by slightly rephrasing it in your own words, keeping the original intent.

When you display and discuss a slide during a live presentation, the headline is a starting point, and you should add value with the commentary you provide as you explain the visual evidence on the slide. Direct your audience's attention to the slide when needed while focusing on maintaining eye contact with your audience rather than the screen.

Not Every Slide Needs a Headline

You may use a mix of topic headings, question headings, and headlines within the same deck. While most content slides benefit from a clear headline, you will find cases where a headline may not be necessary. For example, slides that present detailed financial data—such as balance sheets or quarterly earnings—often serve a reference function rather than advancing a specific point. In these cases, a simple topic heading like *Q4 Financial Summary* may be more appropriate than a headline.

A popular online discussion board has a thread dedicated to headlines where it's clear that some people have very strong opinions on the use of headlines—both in favor of and against:

- It doesn't matter whether you like using headlines, what matters is whether your audience finds them helpful.

- Don't force them. For example, if you are presenting a timeline for an upcoming project, use the topic heading: "Timeline" rather than "This is the timeline for the project." However, if you are mid-project and ahead of schedule, it might be helpful to surface that point in the heading with this headline: "We are ahead of schedule."

Once you've decided on your heading, you may find that some slides need a little extra support in the form of a subheading.

Decide Whether to Add a Sub-Headline

Directly beneath a slide's main heading, you may consider including a sub-headline. A sub-headline provides you with the opportunity to clarify, expand, or frame the main point. The font size of the sub-headline text is typically a smaller font size than the heading text.[*]

When you use a sub-headline, you can select one of three main approaches: a topic heading with a sub-headline, a question heading with sub-headline, or a headline with sub-headline.

Topic Headings and Sub-Headlines

Consider using a *topic heading* with a sub-headline when you anticipate that the audience expects topic headings and you think they would value a sub-headline that surfaces the main point of the slide.

---

* While some people use the term *subheading* to refer to any smaller title on a slide, this book uses the term *sub-headline* to describe a specific element beneath the main heading. Segment headings, introduced in the next chapter, appear in the body of the slide.

Let's consider three examples where including a topic heading followed by a sub-headline might be appropriate throughout a slide deck:

1. Consulting slide decks often include common topic headings and sub-headlines with content tailored to the specific client engagement.

   - Example Slide 1
     - Topic Heading: Project Scope
     - Sub-headline: Key focus areas include process optimization and stakeholder engagement.
   - Example Slide 2
     - Topic Heading: Goals & Objectives
     - Sub-headline: Achieve operational efficiency and improve customer satisfaction.
   - Example Slide 3
     - Topic Heading: Success Metrics
     - Sub-headline: Key performance indicators include cost savings and revenue growth.

2. A real estate market analysis often includes slides with similar topic headings like market overview, demographic analysis, and economic indicators.

   - Example Slide 1
     - Topic Heading: Market Overview
     - Sub-headline: Ithaca's real estate market benefits from consistent demand fueled by Cornell University and a growing local economy.
   - Example Slide 2
     - Topic Heading: Demographic Analysis
     - Sub-headline: Ithaca's median age, household size, and income levels highlight a strong need for rental properties and affordable housing options.

- Example Slide 3
  - ▸ Topic Heading: Economic Indicators
  - ▸ Sub-headline: Local economic growth is supported by higher education, healthcare, and tourism sectors.

3. Pitch decks often include conventional topic headings on slides like problem, solution, and market. In these situations, consider including a topic heading that investors expect and a brief sub-headline that communicates each of those slides' main points.

- Example Slide 1
  - ▸ Topic Heading: Problem
  - ▸ Sub-headline: Current snack options are often high in sugar and fail to meet the needs of health-conscious consumers.
- Example Slide 2
  - ▸ Topic Heading: Solution
  - ▸ Sub-headline: Our trail mix delivers great taste, balanced nutrition, and perfectly portioned packs for modern lifestyles.
- Example Slide 3
  - ▸ Topic Heading: Market
  - ▸ Sub-headline: Health-conscious consumers and busy professionals are fueling growth in the better-for-you snack category.

These examples share a common strategy: The audience expects familiar signposts in the heading. In each case, topic headings provide a predictable structure, while the sub-headline surfaces the main point of the slide. This pairing can quickly orient your audience.

Now let's look at another option: pairing a question heading with a sub-headline.

Question Headings and Sub-Headlines

Consider including a *question heading* followed by a sub-headline in two situations.

- Include a question heading and sub-headline when you want to elicit a discussion and include the answer to the question. Here's how you might apply this strategy: Build in animation that allows the sub-headline to appear once you click advance on your clicker or the forward arrow on your keyboard.

  1. Ask the question.
  2. Allow for some engagement with your audience.
  3. Display the answer.

- Include a question heading followed by the answer in the sub-headline when creating a frequently-asked-questions document where each slide includes one question and the answer.

Headlines and Sub-Headlines

A headline followed by a sub-headline can be particularly helpful when designing a high-density deck that will need to make stand-alone sense. Because a slide heading provides limited space, a sub-headline, which serves as a textual bridge between the headline and the graphic and textual elements in the slide body, enables you to surface key commentary in any of three ways:

- **Summarize**: Use sub-headlines to summarize the information displayed on the slide. If you think of a heading as if it is a newspaper headline that makes a succinct main point, your sub-headline could be a more extensive summary of the information in the slide body.

- **Make a point**: Use sub-headlines to elaborate on the main idea the headline conveys. If you think of the headline as if it is a heading in a formal report, your sub-headline functions like a topic sentence for the introductory paragraph.

- **Introduce evidence**: Use sub-headlines to introduce evidence in support of the point that the headline conveys. If you think of the headline as if it's an assertion, you can use the sub-headline to highlight key data that the slide body displays.

Let's look at one example headline and see these three different approaches in action. In a presentation about active listening, a headline might read: Active listening builds stronger relationships.

- **Sub-headline that includes a summary**: "It increases trust, reduces misunderstandings, and strengthens connections." This example provides a concise summary of what follows on the slide.

- **Sub-headline that makes a point**: "By understanding others, we create deeper emotional bonds and improve collaboration." This example sub-headline continues the point made in the headline.

- **Sub-headline that introduces evidence**: "Studies show that teams practicing active listening are more effective at resolving conflicts." This example sub-headline introduces evidence to substantiate the claim made in the headline.

Most of the same guidance that applies to writing headlines applies to writing sub-headlines, except sub-headlines

1. Should extend to no more than three lines of text
2. Should include end punctuation

The sub-headline should not repeat the heading.

Consider Using Trackers

In some situations, you may want to include three levels of information in the upper-left area of the slide. You've already seen how headings and sub-headlines work. The third level—called a tracker—can guide your audience through a more complex deck.

A tracker is typically a word or phrase that identifies the current section of the deck. It often matches—or is a concise version of—the text used in the table of contents or on the section-divider slides. Trackers are usually formatted differently from headings. They are in smaller text, sometimes in ALL CAPS or a lighter color (such as grayscale), to visually distinguish them from the main heading and sub-headline. You'll find more guidance on placement and formatting of trackers in the *polishing* section of the book.

For example, consider a common structure used in real estate offering memorandums. These slide decks often include sections such as *Executive Summary, Investment Highlights, Property Overview, Market Overview*, and *Financial Summary*. On the content slides within each section, a tracker with the respective section name could be placed above the heading, helping the audience know where they are in the overall structure of the deck.

This practice isn't limited to real estate. In a deck from Ernst & Young that focuses on global power and utilities deals, each section—such as *Overview, Technology Investment Trends, Americas*, and *Asia-Pacific*—is labeled with a tracker in the upper-left corner of the content slides.

Match Your Heading to Your Slide's Information Density

The type of heading you use should support how much information appears on the slide. While there's no one "right" match, the table below offers general guidelines based on how much content your audience will need to process.

Pairing Heading Types with Information Density Level

Heading Type	Best for Information Density
Topic heading (with no sub-headline)	Low
Topic heading with a sub-headline	Medium to High
Headline (with no sub-headline)	Low to Medium
Headline with a sub-headline	High

These are not hard rules, but they reflect how different heading types can support audience comprehension. When your slide contains minimal content, a concise heading—either a topic or a headline—is often sufficient. As slides become denser, a sub-headline can help clarify the core message.

Chapter 5 Takeaways

- Use message headings—also called headlines—to state the slide's takeaway.
- Choose topic or question headings when the purpose is to introduce or invite reflection, not conclude.
- Message headings improve comprehension, retention, and alignment across team members.
- If your audience will read the slides (before, during, or after a presentation), clarity in the heading becomes essential.
- Use ellipses sparingly to connect ideas across slides when building a narrative flow.
- Sub-headlines can clarify the main idea, especially when topic or question headings are used.

Headlines and sub-headlines are intended to *tell* your points. In the next chapter, we'll explore how to identify the right supporting information and *show* in the form of graphics and text.

Determine Supporting Information

Grace was a rising associate at a prominent investment bank, known for her sharp modeling skills and meticulous deal memos. So, when she was asked to create a slide deck for an upcoming client pitch, she opened her slide software with confidence.

She knew the numbers inside and out. The valuation assumptions were tight. The comps were clean. And as she'd done dozens of times before, she started typing: heading at the top, bullet points below. Then more bullets. Then a table. Then a chart. By the end of the day, she had built what felt like a solid deck. It was dense and detailed. It looked like decks she'd seen senior bankers present.

But during the internal review, a managing director flipped through the deck and paused. "Grace, the data's solid," he said, "but this reads like a Word doc. Where's the story? What should the client actually *see*?"

Grace froze. She had built the deck the only way she knew—by starting with text. No one had ever taught her how to design a slide with a clear main point and persuasive visual support.

She's not alone.

———————————————■———————————————

In finance, and in many other fields, many professionals use bullet points as the default approach to supporting ideas. They're fast to write and familiar to read. But that default leads too many professionals to skip an essential question: *What's the best way to support the main point atop the slide?*

Too often, the answer becomes "text." And so, we fall into patterns encouraged by the software itself. You click "Add Text." A bullet point appears. Then another. And before long, you've built a wall of words.

Of course, the software isn't the only culprit. Outdated slide design rules reinforce the habit. Ever heard of the 4×4 Rule? No more than four bullet points per slide, no more than four words per line. Or maybe you've come across the 6×6, 7×7, or even the 8×8 Rule. Each prescribes a different magic number of bullet points and words per line. Some business communication textbooks still advocate for the 6×2 Rule, which allows six bullets, each up to two lines long. That's 12 lines of text— essentially a paragraph disguised as a slide.

In 2005, Cliff Atkinson emerged as an early voice calling for a different approach. His book *Beyond Bullet Points* challenged the default reliance on bulleted slides, arguing that presenters should build structured, story-driven presentations.[1] But decades later, the struggle persists.

To be clear, bullet points aren't the enemy. Used appropriately and in moderation, they can organize information effectively. The problem is that rules about how many bullet points to use focus on the wrong thing. And telling people to "use fewer bullet points" isn't enough.

The real question isn't *how many to use*—it's *what is the best way to support my main point?*

This chapter answers that question.

You'll learn a process for moving beyond a text-first mindset. Along the way, you'll see why a visual-first approach helps your audience not only understand more but remember more too.

Why Text-Heavy Slides Frustrate Audiences

When slides that accompany a live presentation are overloaded with text, audiences are forced to read and listen at the same time. This is a cognitive multitasking nightmare. Gene Zelazny explains that presenters have three bad options when dealing with text-heavy slides:

1. Read the words verbatim. (Audiences dislike being read to.)
2. Paraphrase the text. (Audiences struggle to read and listen at the same time.)
3. Let them read in silence. (Audiences find this awkward.)[2]

None of these scenarios lead to a successful presentation. But how audiences react is even more telling:

1. Some ignore the slides and listen to you.
2. Some ignore you and focus on reading the slide.
3. Some check out altogether.

High-density slides interfere with comprehension—especially during live presentations. Text-heavy slides create competing streams of information, forcing your audience to choose between reading and listening. And even when you design a slide that is meant to be read independently, excessive text still poses a challenge. Dense blocks of writing can slow readers down and discourage otherwise motivated readers.

When I show workshop participants three versions of the same slide: low-, medium-, and high-density—they often tell me that their organization's "normal" is far denser than the highest-density example. And that example already represents the upper word count limit of what I'd recommend for a content slide.

Experts like Garr Reynolds advocate for limiting or eliminating bullet points altogether, emphasizing simplicity and imagery.[3] His advice is great for ballroom-style presentations—like TED Talks and keynote addresses—where the speaker's words and presence do the heavy lifting.

But those aren't the type of presentations that work well in meetings used to drive decision-making.

Most professionals aren't delivering polished, minimalist keynote speeches. Those individuals need slides that do more than look sleek on the big screen.

You need a different set of strategies. Instead of defaulting to words, start by identifying the main point of the slide and then consider what graphic (or graphics) will help support the main idea of the slide. Only after choosing the right visual support should you decide if (and how much) text is needed to enhance clarity.

At the simplest level, you have three options:

1. Graphic support[4]

2. Textual support

3. A mix of graphic and textual support

For most workplace decks, you'll need a mix of graphics and text to support your main points. Rather than starting with text, you should consider taking a visual-first approach.

Remember: Your goal shouldn't be to fill the slide; your goal should be to support your message.

Before we discuss what to include in the body of a slide, let's consider in a bit more detail why a visual-first approach can lead to better results.

Take a Visual-First Approach

For over two decades in my communication courses, I've asked students to draft a slide deck before delivering their presentations. That means I've seen thousands of presentations in progress, and almost all of them start the same way. Bullet points. More bullet points. I've observed the same pattern in my executive education workshops, where employees at all levels build slides in real time. People rarely start with graphics. At some point, though, they realize that what they are making looks more like a document than a slide deck.

Why does this happen? Because most people default to text. It feels familiar. It's easy. Typing seems like progress. And when a topic is complex, people often worry they'll oversimplify the message or, worse, omit some important idea. So, they compensate—with words, and lots of them.

While text may be easier for you to put on a slide, it's not easy for your audience to absorb.

Flip the default. Instead of starting with text, ask yourself, What's the best way to show this? Think diagrams, charts, images. Text isn't the enemy, but it works best when it plays a supporting role to visuals.

Why Visuals Work

Imagine someone handed you a deck with ten slides filled with dense text. No headlines. No charts. No diagrams. Just paragraph after paragraph of explanation. How long before your eyes start to glaze over? Now imagine they hand you a deck on the same topic, but this time the points are made in headlines, and those points are supported by graphics. Suddenly, the same information is easier to process and easier to remember.

Why do visuals work so well? Two well-documented cognitive effects help explain the advantage:

- Visuals are easier for audiences to process (according to dual-coding theory).
- Visuals are easier for audiences to remember (due to the picture-superiority effect).

The human brain retains visual images with astonishing accuracy. In 1970, University of Rochester psychologist Ralph Haber ran an experiment in which he showed people 2,560 pictures, then tested how many they could recall later. Participants remembered 85 to 95 percent—a staggering rate. It was as if the brain had a built-in camera that could store visuals. While Haber didn't directly compare pictures to words, his findings helped establish how accurately we remember images.[5]

Meanwhile, around 200 miles west in Canada, psychologist Allan Paivio at the University of Western Ontario explored how the brain processes information. He developed dual-coding theory, which suggested that the brain stores words and images in two separate systems. Pictures get encoded twice—once as an image and again with a verbal label.

Words, on the other hand, only get encoded once.[6] These findings suggest that visuals can be more intuitive to process than text. (However, whether visuals are processed faster than text remains unclear.)[7]

Not long after Paivio first published dual-coding theory, another group of researchers from the University of South Florida wanted to know if pictures are only better because we mentally give them verbal labels. Or do they have an advantage even when no words are involved? They found that even when people didn't label the picture in their heads, they still remember them better than words.[8] In short: Images are better because they stick in our minds in ways words don't. This is known as picture superiority effect.[9]

Recent research has popularized the picture-superiority effect. John Medina, a molecular biologist and author of *Brain Rules*, found that people remember 65 percent of visual information three days after being exposed to it, but only 10 percent of text.[10]

Let's try to see this in action. Take 15 seconds to study the image below. Try to memorize both the words and the pictures.

| | Octopus | | Snake | | Cat |
| Skunk | | Giraffe | | Turtle |

Write down as many animals as you remember—whether you saw them as pictures or as words.

Now reflect: Which did you remember more easily? Most people recall more of the pictures than the words—even when they're not trying to. This is the picture-superiority effect at work. Our brains are simply wired to retain images more effectively than text.

Which Slide Would You Prefer?

Leaner staffing lowered cost per guest

Leaner staffing model

Reducing baseline staffing during nonpeak hours helped control labor costs without compromising service. Instead of staffing based on fixed coverage templates, managers used historical demand patterns to build more flexible rosters. For example, some locations shifted from static morning and evening shifts to staggered start times, better aligning hours worked with guest volume. These changes also made scheduling more adaptable in response to real-time fluctuations. As one of our managers noted, "The goal isn't fewer people—it's the right people, at the right time."

Cross-trained employees

Empowering employees to take on multiple responsibilities enabled greater operational agility. For instance, front-desk staff trained to assist with concierge tasks and food runners who could support housekeeping during turnover periods made it easier to maintain service quality without additional head count. Cross-training also helped reduce idle time by allowing employees to pivot based on guest flow and priority needs. A recent industry survey found that 68% of operators who cross-trained reported improvements in shift productivity.

Optimized resource allocation

Aligning labor, supplies, and services more closely with actual demand led to a measurable drop in cost per guest. Teams used simple forecasting tools—sometimes just spreadsheets based on prior-year trends—to adjust staffing levels and reduce waste. For example, instead of pre-staging full amenities on all floors, supply distribution was adjusted dynamically based on room occupancy. This shift not only cut costs but also improved inventory management across departments.

Leaner staffing lowered cost per guest

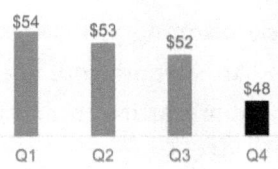

Leaner staffing model: Reduced baseline staffing levels during nonpeak hours helped lower total labor spend.

Cross-trained employees: Teams covered multiple functions without adding head count, improving efficiency per shift.

Optimized resource allocation: Efforts to match labor, supplies, and services to actual guest demand helped lower cost per guest.

When I share similar comparisons in my executive education workshops, the consensus is clear: Most readers, especially managerial- and executive-level, prefer the second slide.

The first slide presents detailed information using full paragraphs. While it captures nuance, the volume of text is too much, making it difficult to scan quickly. The second slide presents a chart alongside key takeaways, making the content easier to process.

How to Think Visually

Taking an idea that you've thought about and written down in text and converting that idea into a graphical representation isn't easy. One reason why it's particularly challenging for many of us is that we lack what visual-storytelling expert Dan Roam calls *visual grammar*. He suggests that, in our educational system, we develop *verbal grammar* with our emphasis on words, but most of us never develop the equivalent skill set for visual thinking. This leaves us feeling uncertain when we attempt to express our ideas in something other than text.

The good news is that visual thinking is a skill you can learn. If you want to explore visual storytelling in more detail, Roam's work—particularly *Blah Blah Blah*—is an excellent resource.[11] His approach contributed to how I think about visual communication. In this chapter, though, you'll learn a process designed to help you think visually when creating slide decks.

If you created a storyboard during the planning process, you may already have an idea of how you intend to support your ideas. But whether you're beginning with a storyboard or starting from scratch, it helps to follow a consistent process. In the next few pages, you'll learn how to decide what kind of support each slide needs and how to choose the best way to present that support visually.

The four-step process will help you make those decisions with more confidence:

1. Determine the main point of the slide.
2. Select the right category of graphic to support your point.
3. Select the most effective type of graphic and number of graphics to support your point.
4. Add text—only if necessary—to support, illustrate, or interpret your message.

Step 1: Determine the Main Point of the Slide

Before you think about visuals, you need to determine the main point of the slide. (Remember my advice from the last chapter?) Ask yourself, If my audience only remembers one thing from this slide, what should it be?

Think of your main point like the topic sentence of a paragraph. When you start reading a paragraph, you make a quick judgment—Is this relevant? Do you want to keep reading the entire paragraph? Skim it? Or skip ahead? Your audience does the same thing with slides. Every time you advance to a new slide (or your audience scrolls to the next slide while reading), they glance at the heading and decide: Does this matter to me? Do I want to keep going? If the point seems relevant, they will expect supporting details.

Step 2: Select the Right Category of Graphic

Determine what graphic category can best support the point you make in the heading. At first glance, this step may seem unnecessary, but the goal is to break down the process of thinking visually into smaller parts. The following tables show how different types of headings align with common audience questions and graphic categories.

Topic headings are often used to introduce concepts, processes, or data. The first table maps each type to likely questions and helpful graphic categories.

Topic Headings Categories

Heading	Audience Question	Graphic Category
Concept-Oriented	What is X? Why does X matter?	• Conceptual & Explanatory • Image-Based
Process-Oriented	How does it work?	• Process & Sequence • Relationship
Data-Oriented	What does the data show?	• Data • Context & Location

Question headings can serve different rhetorical functions. The next table links common question heading types with the kinds of graphics that best support each heading type.

Question Heading Categories

Heading	Audience Question	Graphic Category
Focus Attention	Why does this matter?	• Data • Image-Based
Encourage Engagement	What do you think?	• Image-Based • Relationship
Frame the Discussion	How should we think about this?	• Relationship • Conceptual & Explanatory
Organize the Content	Where do we start?	• Process & Sequence • Context & Location

Message headings (headlines) convey insight, conclusions, or recommendations. The following table shows how each type aligns with audience needs and typical graphic choices.

Message Heading Categories

Heading	Audience Question	Graphic Category
Insight-Oriented	What's the big idea?	• Conceptual & Explanatory • Context & Location
Conclusion-Oriented	What does this mean?	• Data • Process & Sequence
Recommendation-Oriented	What should we do?	• Process & Sequence • Relationship

Step 3: Select the Most Effective Type of Graphic

Now that you have an idea of the category of graphics to support your point, select the specific type of graphic appropriate for your point. Consider these questions:

- What graphic makes the takeaway instantly clear?
- How much detail does the audience need to see at a glance?

As you consider your options, remember that the following list is intended to assist in the process rather than be rules to follow. From what I've seen in my research on workplace slide decks, the categories of graphics below are listed from most frequently used to least.

Data graphics display numerical information, trends, and comparisons.

- **Bar and column charts:** Compare quantities across different categories.
- **Line graphs:** Show trends over time.
- **Pie charts:** Illustrate proportions of a whole.
- **Scatter plots:** Display correlations or patterns between two variables.
- **Tables:** Present precise numerical or categorial comparisons.

Process and sequence graphics illustrate sequence, steps, and transformations.

- **Timelines:** Present chronological events, project phases, or milestone tracking.

- **Flowcharts:** Map out decision-making processes, workflows, or procedural steps.
- **Chevron diagrams:** Show a structured sequence of steps in a process.
- **Gantt charts:** Display project timelines and dependencies.
- **Cycle diagrams:** Illustrate continuous or repeating processes.

Relationship graphics show relationships between concepts, ideas, or structures.

- **T-charts and pros/cons tables:** Compare two options side by side to highlight differences and trade-offs.
- **Pyramid diagrams:** Represent hierarchical relationships or rankings.
- **Venn diagrams:** Illustrate areas of overlap and distinction between two or more elements.
- **Side-by-side images:** Contrast before-and-after scenarios or competing approaches visually.

Conceptual and explanatory graphics explain abstract ideas, models, or concepts.

- **Concept diagrams:** Break down abstract ideas into visual components.
- **Representational illustrations:** Clarify the structure or function of physical objects, systems, or mechanisms.
- **Metaphorical images:** Visual representations that convey abstract ideas through symbolic forms—such as a bridge for connection, a ladder for growth, or a mountain for challenges.

Context and location graphics situate information about place, time, or space.

- **Maps:** Show geographic distribution, trends, or location.
- **Calendar-based graphics:** Highlight key dates, schedules, or project milestones.

Image-based graphics enhance comprehension through real and symbolic representations.

- **Photographs**: Show real-world applications, people, or settings for credibility and emotional impact.
- **Icons**: Simplify abstract ideas into recognizable visual symbols.

You have many options when it comes to supporting your point with graphics. And it's worth noting that many effective graphics *include* text. But instead of presenting that text in sentence or list form, the information becomes part of the graphic itself. A table, a flowchart, a labeled photo—each blends visuals and words to create something that's easier to scan, absorb, and remember.

Try This with AI

Brainstorm visual-first options. *Prompt:* "What are three different ways I could visualize this idea or data? [Describe the main idea or metric you want to show.]"

How do you decide if more than one graphic is necessary on a slide? This is not an easy question to answer, so I will begin to address it here and provide more guidance in the next chapter. For now, let two factors guide you.

First, consider the level of information density your audience expects. The lower the density, the fewer graphics you should use. The next table offers general guidance for how many support graphics are typically appropriate based on slide density.

Number of Graphics

Content-Slide Type	Optimal Number of Support Graphics	Guidance
Low-Density	1	Use one strong graphic.
Medium-Density	1–2	Use one or two graphics if they are distinct and work together.
High-Density	1–4	Use multiple graphics only if needed.

In a study I conducted with my graduate student Roberto Teran, we analyzed investor presentations from publicly traded companies and found that content slides typically included about two graphics on average—but most commonly, individual slides have just one. Low-density slides should include one strong focal point, while high-density slides can support multiple graphics if they're laid out well.[12]

Second, consider the ease with which your audience will process the different categories of graphics. For example, it's much easier to process two image-based graphics (e.g., photographs) than two conceptual graphics (e.g., concept diagrams). I am not aware of research that has specifically compared the ease with which different graphic categories are processed, but several cognitive theories suggest that our brains process visual information in a hierarchical manner, from simple to complex forms.

Although ease of processing shouldn't be your primary reason for choosing a graphic type, it's a useful factor to consider when adding more than one graphic to a slide.

Based on my review of empirical research, I propose the following list—from requiring the least cognitive resources to the most.

1. **Image-based graphics:** If you've ever glanced at a road sign and instantly recognized the symbol for "Stop" or "Airport," you've experience dual-coding theory in action.[13] When you see a familiar image, your brain recognizes and interprets it almost instantly. Photographs and symbols tap into cognitive shortcuts that help you absorb information with minimal effort.

2. **Data graphics:** Well-designed charts and graphics—those that use visual features like color, shape, and orientation to make a trend stand out—require almost no effort by your brain to process. These graphics use pre-attentive cues (a fancy way of saying your brain notices certain visual elements before you're even aware you are looking at them) to guide attention.[14]

3. **Relationship graphics:** Your brain is great at spotting simple things like a bright red dot in a sea of blue ones, without even trying. But when you need to compare options—like picking the best investment, vendor, or software—a bit more cognitive effort is required. Feature integration theory finds your brain doesn't automatically connect the dots between multiple features (like price, reliability, customer ratings). Instead, you have to focus on one at a time and piece them together, which takes effort.[15]

4. **Process and sequence graphics:** Timelines and process workflows aren't something you can absorb in a single glance (just ask anyone who's ever tried to assemble IKEA furniture without losing their mind). According to cognitive load theory, when you have to process a sequence of steps, it puts serious strain on your working memory. The more complex the sequence, the harder it is to hold on to previous steps while making sense of the new one.[16]

5. **Context and location graphics:** Our brains process maps and schedules differently from other types of visuals. According to research by Barbara Tversky of Stanford University, people build mental shortcuts—simplifying distances, exaggerating key landmarks, and aligning roads in ways that make sense to us, even if they're technically wrong. That's why context graphics like maps and schedules require you to mentally place yourself in the environment to interpret distance, routes, and locations.[17]

6. **Conceptual and explanatory graphics:** Concept graphics aren't something you can just glance at and immediately understand. These graphics force us to wrestle with ideas, making them the most cognitively demanding category of all. Constructivist

learning theory suggests learning is an active process in which you connect new ideas to what you already know.[18] That's why frameworks like the Four Ps of Marketing or Maslow's Hierarchy of Needs take effort to understand. You're not just seeing information, you're interpreting relationships, applying prior knowledge, and trying to make sense of how it all fits together.

If multiple graphics are necessary, be sure each one adds a different layer of meaning and that your audience can process them both easily.

If you identify more graphics than you find are reasonable to include on one slide (either given the level of information density you are aiming for or the expected difficulty your audience will have processing the information at once), you have at least two options:

1. Pick the graphic that most strongly supports your point and omit the other(s).

2. Narrow the scope of the slide. Reframe the heading to make a point that the first graphic supports and create a subsequent slide that makes a point that the second graphic supports.

Step 4: Add Textual Support (only when necessary)

Once you've selected the best graphic(s) to support your main point, you may find that text is still needed to enhance clarity, reinforce key ideas, or guide interpretation.

Even with a graphic, there's something about empty space on a slide that compels people to fill it.

As you consider what text to add, you need to be intentional. Only use text that's truly necessary. And to do that, follow four steps:

- Step 4A: Determine if textual support is needed at all.
- Step 4B: Identify what explanatory text needs to do.
- Step 4C: Choose the best form of explanatory text.
- Step 4D: Add additional text elements.

Step 4A: Determine If Textual Support Is Needed at All

Before adding text, ask yourself:

1. Does the graphic need text to be understood?
2. Would key information be misinterpreted without text?
3. Does the audience need additional context to process the slide efficiently?

The answer to these questions depends on the role the slide deck will play in the communication situation you are preparing it for. The table below outlines how that role should influence your decision to include—or omit—text.

Textual Support

If the slide deck will ...	The graphic ...
Support a speaker during a live presentation	May not need textual support because the presenter can provide it orally.
Be read	Will likely need textual support because a presenter won't be there to explain it.
Be used during a live presentation and need to make sense to audiences before or after a presentation (without a presenter)	Will likely need some level of textual support—enough to stand alone without becoming distracting or excessive during live delivery.

If you answered "no" to the three questions above, then congratulations! You just saved yourself some time and your audience from unnecessary text. Move on to your next slide. But if the answer is "yes," your next move is to figure out what the text needs to do.

Step 4B: Identify What the Text Needs to Do

Text can support, illustrate, and/or interpret the content of the slide. If text isn't serving one of these purposes, it's probably just taking up space. Delete it. That means you need to approach the text with a critical eye: no text that repeats the slide heading, no filler text to make the slide feel full, and no generic statements that don't add value.

Support

Use text to provide evidence, credibility, and context for the point you make in the headline.

- **Present evidence:** Substantiate your argument with statistics, data points, or research findings.
- **Build credibility:** Quote or paraphrase experts or refer to authoritative sources.
- **Provide context:** Situate your argument with background information.

Use text to support your point when your audience needs additional information to understand or trust your point.

Slide decks can include links to external resources. To enhance your credibility and help your reader find additional information, include links to third-party information. A link embedded into text is more aesthetically pleasing and doesn't take up as much space as a URL typed out. Of course, this strategy only works for slide decks where the audience has a digital copy (rather than a slide deck that is presented or shared as a hard copy).

Illustrate

Use text to make your point more vivid or concrete.

- **Give examples:** Make your point concrete with anecdotes or real-life case studies.
- **Make comparisons:** Improve audience understanding with analogies that simplify complex concepts or make them more relatable.
- **Add descriptions:** Make abstract ideas easier to understand with details that paint a clear picture for the audience.

Use text to illustrate when you want to make your point more memorable, emotionally engaging, or easier to grasp.

Interpret

Use text to explain or analyze.

- **Draw conclusions:** Explain what the data means and why it matters.
- **Clarify trends:** Highlight key patterns and what they reveal.
- **Add captions or annotations:** Guide the audience with brief explanations.

Use text to interpret when the audience might miss the significance of a point without additional explanation.

You may interpret graphics by placing explanatory text and annotations above, below, beside, or embedded within the graphic elements. You can find more detailed guidance about annotations in chapter 9.

Step 4C: Choose the Best Form of Explanatory Text

Now that you understand the various ways text can support, illustrate, and interpret your points, it's time to consider how much text to use.

Most people get into trouble when trying to decide the best form of explanatory text. Once you start adding text, it's easy to keep going. A phrase turns into a sentence. A sentence turns into a paragraph. Suddenly, your slide is drowning in words.

The form of explanatory text you use should align with the overall density of the slide. Different levels of information density call for different approaches to text. As shown in the table below, you should tailor your explanatory text to match the information density of your slide.

Explanatory Text

Content-Slide Type	Best Form of Explanatory Text
Low-density	A single word and brief phrases
Medium-density	Brief phrases and short sentences
High-density	Short sentences and concise paragraphs

You have a few tools at your disposal:

- A single word
- A brief phrase
- A complete sentence
- A brief paragraph
- A bulleted or numbered list

Each form of explanatory text offers a different level of detail to help you support your points effectively.

A single word: The right word can clarify meaning, evoke emotion, or leave a memorable impression. Use a single word when you need to label, name, or emphasize a single idea. A stand-alone word is a great way to capture attention. Think of Steve Jobs unveiling a new project with a single word on the slide: *Revolutionary*. Use this technique when presenting a low-density slide.

A brief phrase: A phrase can summarize ideas or convey nuance. Use a phrase when a single word is too brief to support your point, but a full sentence would be unnecessary. Phrases are short but meaningful, making them ideal for high-skim-value content. Consider using action-oriented phrases (e.g., "Increase customer retention" instead of "Retention strategies"). Phrases are great for low- and medium-density decks.

A complete sentence: A well-crafted sentence helps your audience understand your point. Include a complete thought to improve clarity. Keep sentences short (i.e., avoid long or multi-clause sentences). Brief sentences are most appropriate on medium- to high-density slides.

A brief paragraph: A paragraph provides you with the opportunity to group related ideas. Use a paragraph when you need to add details or offer a more thorough explanation. Limit each paragraph to no more than three or four lines of text. If needed, break up longer paragraphs into brief ones. Brief paragraphs are most appropriate in high-density decks, where the explanatory text enables each slide to make stand-alone sense—and address questions likely to emerge in the readers' minds without a presenter needing to add oral commentary.

Content slides are not the place for lengthy paragraphs or a series of uninterrupted paragraphs. Instead of using a long prose passage, consider using graphic elements, separate briefer paragraphs, and bulleted lists.

The slide below contains over 250 words arranged in uninterrupted paragraphs, making it difficult to scan and absorb. Without graphics or structural breaks, it feels like reading a wall of text. If your audience wanted paragraphs, they would have requested a traditional business report. Breaking the content into shorter paragraphs, bulleted lists, or adding graphic elements can improve readability and retention.

This slide has way too much text

This slide has way too much text. This slide has way too much text. This slide has way too much text. This slide has way too much text. This slide has way too much text. This slide has way too much text. This slide has way too much text. This slide has way too much text. This slide has way too much text. This slide has way too much text. This slide has way too much text. This slide has way too much text.

This slide has way too much text. This slide has way too much text. This slide has way too much text. This slide has way too much text. This slide has way too much text. This slide has way too much text. This slide has way too much text. This slide has way too much text. This slide has way too much text. This slide has way too much text. This slide has way too much text.

This slide has way too much text. This slide has way too much text. This slide has way too much text. This slide has way too much text. This slide has way too much text. This slide has way too much text. This slide has way too much text. This slide has way too much text. This slide has way too much text. This slide has way too much text. This slide has way too much text. This slide has way too much text.

A bulleted or numbered list: When you are discussing two or more ideas that are functionally equivalent, a list provides you with the opportunity to organize information into easily digestible units.

Bulleted lists get a bad rap. Because they are the default way of adding content in most slide presentation software, slide deck creators tend to over-rely on them. Edward Tufte points out that bulleted lists can promote shallow thinking and fragmented information. And while Steve Jobs may not have used bullet points on his slides during Apple's product launches, most of us aren't giving keynote presentations that will influence how humans communicate across the globe.

Consider the following guidance to make sure you're using lists appropriately.

Make certain that listed items are functionally equivalent. In other words, all items in a list should belong to the same logical category. Examples of functionally equivalent items may be a list of benefits, goals, features, key points, or a sequence of steps in a process.

Introduce each list with a concise phrase or sentence. A clear lead-in can serve several functions:

- **Set context:** Explain the purpose of the list and how it relates to the main point of the slide. For example, "These are the benefits of active listening" signals why the list matters and how it supports the broader message.
- **Establish expectations:** Help the audience anticipate the type and number of items to follow. For example, "Here are five strategies for paraphrasing" cues both the content and the structure of the list.
- **Clarify relationships:** Show how the items relate to one another and the overall message—whether they are sequential steps, equally weighted options, or subpoints categorized under a larger theme. For example, "Active listening consists of three key skills, each building on the previous one" shows a sequential relationship.

Keep lists concise by trying to limit them to three to four items. Research on cognitive load and working memory shows that people can comfortably process only a small number of items at a time. However, if you have more than four points, you have a few choices:

- **Combine ideas.** Look for ways to group related ideas under a single bullet point.
- **Spread the points across multiple lists or slides.** Break your content into smaller sections. For example, if you have eight strategies in a list, you could break them into two lists of four, one for short-term strategies and one for long-term strategies.

- **Exceed four bullet points.** If combining or spreading ideas isn't feasible, keep all the points in the same list. For example, if you were presenting the Big Five personality traits—a framework used to describe individual differences—omitting or condensing traits would undermine the model and confuse the audience. A better option would be to introduce all five traits on one slide, then dedicate a separate slide to each trait if deeper explanation is required.

Begin each point with parallel phrasing. Parallel phrasing means using consistent grammatical structure for each item in a series. For example, consider these items that we might place in a bulleted list on a slide: increasing revenue, reducing costs, and improving efficiency. These items are grammatically parallel because each one begins with a verb in the same form.

In contrast, consider these items: increased revenue, cost reduction, and improving efficiency. These items are not grammatically parallel, because the forms are inconsistent. By keeping phrasing consistent, you make items in the list easier to read and understand.

Stick to single-level bullet points. When you keep lists simple and to one level, you improve clarity and readability. Avoid sub-bullets, or even worse, sub-sub-bullets. Multiple levels of bullets can make your slide look cluttered and hard to follow.

Save lists for situations where you need to group clearly distinct points. A common mistake in slide design is turning what should be a paragraph into a series of bullet points. Writers do this by converting each sentence into a bullet—even when the sentences are not distinct ideas. But this approach misuses the list format. Bullet points are meant to organize and highlight separate, discrete ideas, making them easier for your audience to scan and remember. When each bullet simply continues the same thought or elaborates on the previous one, the result is a disjointed list that's difficult to process.

Of course, not everything is best expressed as a list. Keep text in sentence or paragraph form when the ideas flow together in a way that would lose meaning if separated.

Step 4D: Additional Ways to Use Text on Content Slides

Beyond explanatory text, consider if the slide would benefit from segment headings, kickers, and footer information.

Segment Headings

Segment headings are headings that appear in the body area of a content slide, not in the heading or subheading area. Segment headings act as signposts, helping the audience follow the structure of the slide by signaling when a new idea or chunk of information begins. In high-density slides especially, segment headings make it easier for your audience to distinguish between information chunks.[19]

Segment headings typically take one of two forms:

- **Stand-alone:** A heading that appears on its own line, separating it from the content that follows.

- **Call-out:** A heading that appears on the same line as body text that follows and is visually emphasized—often through bold, italics, or color. This type of segment heading "calls out" the key idea at the beginning of line of text.

Like headlines and sub-headlines, segment headings improve the skim value of a slide. Segment headings introduce the content directly beneath them, so that the content doesn't have to do all the explanatory work on its own. These headings may introduce text, graphics, or a combination of text and graphics.

The next slide demonstrates two common ways to use segment headings.

This slide uses stand-alone segment headings to introduce each chart and guide the reader through two key insights. Beneath each chart, supporting explanations are organized using call-out segment headings that emphasize key phrases within the body text.

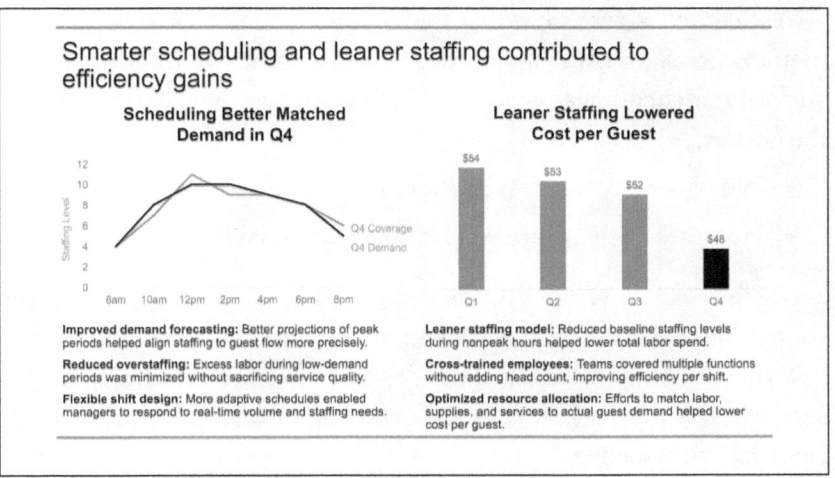

How should you introduce body text and graphics? Now that you understand the two forms of segment headings—stand-alone and call-out—let's turn to the three types of segment headings that shape how your audience interprets the content: topic, question, and message headings. As you learned in chapter 5, when we covered types of slide body headings, each type of segment heading frames the information that follows in a different way.

A *topic segment heading* introduces or labels what follows. Use a topic heading when you want your audience to know *what* follows but you don't want to tell them what to think about it.

- Definition of Self-Awareness
- Key Components of Self-Awareness

A *message segment heading* reveals the main takeaway or insight from the accompanying content. Use a message heading when you want your audience to draw an insight, conclusion, or recommendation from the information that follows.

- Self-Awareness Drives Better Decision-Making
- Understanding Yourself Leads to Better Relationships

A *question segment heading* frames the content that follows as an inquiry. Consider using a question heading when you want to prompt curiosity or encourage reflection—but only when the content provides the answer.

- Why Is Self-Awareness Important?
- How Does Self-Awareness Impact Emotional Intelligence?

Segment headings can also be used to help your audience navigate content by showing how it's grouped or sequenced.

Structural headings divide the slide's body content into clearly labeled sections. Use them when your slide contains two or more distinct categories or perspectives.

- Internal Awareness
- External Awareness

Structural headings function like topic headings but are used in multiples to signal grouping or comparison.

Sequence headings guide the audience through a step-by-step process. These headings can emphasize the order of actions, events, or decisions. Use consistent phrasing (Step 1, Step 2) to make the order clear.

- Step 1: Recognize Your Emotions
- Step 2: Reflect on Their Causes

Does every information chunk need a segment heading? Not every information chunk on a content slide necessarily needs a segment heading, but headings can significantly enhance clarity and organization. Consider adding a segment heading when a chunk introduces a new idea, presents complex or unfamiliar information that benefits from framing, or communicates an insight that deserves emphasis. Segment headings are especially helpful when a slide includes multiple chunks that cover different ideas.

That said, not every chunk requires its own segment heading. You can omit a segment heading when the chunk is clearly tied to the slide headline (or sub-headline) and an additional heading may be redundant.

Likewise, if the entire slide is unified around one main point, inserting an extra segment heading might clutter the layout.

Should all segment headings on a slide follow the same type—like all topic headings or all message headings? Yes, it's generally best to use the same type of segment heading within a slide. Consistency helps your audience process the slide faster. However, there may be cases where mixing segment heading types supports the slide's purpose. For example, a slide about emotional intelligence might include a segment topic heading like *Definition of Emotional Intelligence*, followed by a question segment heading, such as *Why Does It Matter in Leadership?*, and conclude with a message segment heading like *Emotional Intelligence Drives Stronger Team Performance*.

Where should you place a segment heading? A segment heading should typically be placed above the information chunk it refers to. The heading acts as a label that helps the audience quickly understand what they are about to see. This top placement aligns with natural reading patterns (top to bottom). See chapter 9 for details about adding captions to graphic elements.

Kickers

A "kicker" provides one final opportunity to include body text. Kickers typically sit just above the footer, within the main picture frame of a content slide.

Kickers can serve one of three functions:

1. **Takeaway:** A takeaway kicker reinforces the most critical insight or "so what" from the slide. While a headline conveys the primary point of the slide, the takeaway explains why that point matters. It may emphasize what you want the audience to know, believe, decide, act on, or feel. The tone of a takeaway kicker is action oriented.

2. **Summary:** A summary kicker distills the slide's core message into an impactful sentence. If you think about the headline as the topic sentence to a paragraph, you might think about a summary

kicker as the last sentence of a paragraph that ties the content together. The tone of a summary kicker is synthesizing.

3. **Transition:** A transition kicker bridges the current slide to the next. Transitions guide your audience, looking back at what was just covered and looking ahead to what's coming next, or they can simply preview what's next (without looking back). If appropriate for the style of your deck, the tone of a transition kicker can be conversational.

   a. "This is just the beginning. Let's explore how to put these ideas into action."

   b. "With this foundation in place, we're ready to discuss tangible applications."

   c. "Now that we've covered the benefits, let's see how it works in practice."

   The transition should connect rather than repeat, so save the specifics for the upcoming slide.

Consider using a kicker in high-density decks that your audience will read. But if you are preparing a low-density deck that will be presented live, consider omitting the kicker from the slide in favor of speaking aloud the point you want to convey.

Let's see how a kicker works in action. Imagine a content slide with the following headline, sub-headline, and graphic:

- **Headline:** The Pomodoro Technique maximizes focus and efficiency

- **Sub-headline:** Work in focused 25-minute intervals, followed by short breaks, to reduce burnout and boost productivity.

- **Graphic:** A timeline with 25 minutes of work, 5 minutes of break; repeat four times and follow with a 15-minute-long break. Each time period has a different color with labels placed above, and the X-axis shows cumulative time.

Let's consider three different ways a kicker could be used on this slide. The slide's main message stays the same, but depending on the direction you want to take, you could use one of the following kickers:

- **Takeaway:** "Frequent breaks help your brain recharge, keeping you productive all day." This kicker reinforces the primary benefit of the Pomodoro Technique.

- **Summary:** "Structured intervals of work and rest improve efficiency and reduce mental fatigue." This kicker summarizes the core point of the slide in a concise statement.

- **Transition:** "Once you've practiced focused intervals, you'll be ready to turn it into a daily habit." This kicker connects the content on this slide and sets up the content on the next.

A kicker is optional. If you use a kicker on one slide, you don't need to use one on every content slide within the same deck. However, if you choose to use a kicker, consider formatting it consistently throughout.

- Keep the kicker text brief. The best kickers are one line of text, centered at the bottom of the body area of a slide. However, I've occasionally seen effective kickers that extend to three lines of text. Once the kicker text extends beyond two lines, consider aligning it to the left, with a ragged right, rather than centering it.

- Match the text size of the kicker to the text size of the other explanatory text in the slide deck.

- Use black text on a white background, or if you'd like the kicker to stand out a bit more, you might place it in a colored box. For darker-colored boxes, consider using white text rather than black, for easier reading.

- Center the kicker and extend the width to two-thirds of the width of the slide or extend it from margin to margin.

Think of kickers as a tool you have in your toolbox that you don't need to use that often. If you find yourself repeating the headline or sub-headline, then consider omitting the kicker altogether.

Footer Information

The footer is a space for supplemental details that support your slide. A footer is commonly used for citations or disclosures but can serve other functions—all without distracting from the main content.

- **Source citations:** Give credit to data, research, or external information used on the slide.
  - ► Marcus Aurelius. (2006). *Meditations* (G. Hays, Trans.). Modern Library. (Original work published ca. 180 CE)
  - ► Data based on internal company analytics (date)
- **Attribution for graphics:** Credit the creators or sources of images, charts, or other media.
  - ► Image by Getty Images, used with permission.
  - ► Chart adapted from *Harvard Business Review*.
- **Disclaimers:** Protect your organization.
  - ► For internal use only.
  - ► Projections are estimates and not guarantees of future performance.
- **Definitions or clarifications:** Provide additional context for terms or acronyms used on the slide.
  - ► EBITDA: Earnings Before Interest, Taxes, Depreciation, and Amortization.
  - ► YOY: Year-Over-Year
- **Additional information:** Include brief details that aren't critical to the slide's main content but add depth for those who need it.
  - ► Survey conducted with 1,000 respondents.
  - ► Data excludes results from pilot programs.

- **Audience guidance:** Provide instructions for the audience.
  - ▸ Refer to Appendix B for additional data.
  - ▸ Read more about networking here: https://www.andrewquagliata .com/articles/tags/networking.
- **Document control:** Track updates or identify the presentation's version.
  - ▸ Version 3, updated January 9.
  - ▸ Draft—For Review Only.

When designing your template, you should leave room in the footer area of your content slides for supplemental information. Set the size of your footer information to 9 to 11 points.

If the footer information for one slide takes up more space than you've allotted in your content slide template, you may consider the following (preferably in this order):

1. Reduce the size of text.
2. Allow the footer information to extend into the body area of the slide.
3. Embed any website links to reduce the word count of the footnote.
4. Place some of the information in an appendix.

Students and academics accustomed to including references at the end of a document should avoid including a reference slide at the end of the deck. The standard workplace practice is to source information at the bottom of the slide where the reference is used.[20]

If you need to identify the source of supporting evidence, cite your sources as footnotes. Your credibility may rest, in no small part, on the sources of your information.

How to Cite

- Reference credible sources within your text (e.g., According to …).
- Use superscript in order to place a footnote at the end of the sentence.
- Provide the full citation in the footer using a recognized citation style, such as the Harvard Business School Citation Guide.
- Embed URLs into the text if the citation is so long that you run out of space in the footer.

Evaluate Your Supporting Information

I can't tell you which topics, key points, and support to include in your deck. That's where your expertise comes in. However, I can offer a framework to help you decide whether the content you're considering contributes to your message effectively.

As you review your content, ask yourself these questions:

- **Does this align with my purpose?** If your goal is to persuade, does this content actually support your argument or just explain background?

- **Is it relevant to my audience?** Will your audience understand why this matters? Will they care? If not, you may need to reframe it or cut it.

- **Is the takeaway clear?** If someone reads or hears this point, do they know what to conclude, or are you hoping they connect the dots?

- **Is there evidence to support it?** Even compelling ideas lose impact without evidence. Ask yourself: How do I know this is true, and how can I help my audience believe it?

- **Does this add something new?** Especially in dense decks, it's easy to mistake quantity with quality. If something repeats an earlier point, consider cutting it or clarifying what makes it distinct.

Strong slide decks rely on content that is credible. As you evaluate your early thinking, you can adapt a research framework used by many educators and librarians—the CRAAP Test. Originally developed to assess sources, it also works well as a filter for deciding what belongs in your deck.[21]

- **Currency**: Is this data or example recent enough to be persuasive?
- **Relevance**: Will this point matter to this audience in this situation?
- **Authority**: Does this come from a source the audience will find credible?
- **Accuracy**: Is this factually correct and well-supported?
- **Purpose**: Does this support the purpose of my deck or distract from it?

Chapter 6 Takeaways

- Lead with visuals. Start by asking, "What's the best way to show this?"—not "How much text should I add?"
- Match the graphic to the message. Choose a graphic that fits the type of point you're making—concept, process, data, relationship, or context.
- Use multiple graphics only when necessary. Most slides need one strong graphic. Add more only if each adds distinct value and remains easy to process.
- Text should support, not compete. Add text only when it helps the audience understand, remember, or interpret your message.
- Align text to density. Use words, phrases, or short sentences, depending on how much detail your slide needs to convey.

- Use the full toolbox. Segment headings, kickers, and footers can guide attention, reinforce your message, and add credibility.
- Evaluate your supporting content. Keep what advances your purpose, relates to your audience, and is backed by credible evidence.

Now that you've identified the graphic and textual support for your slides, you are ready to lay out your content on the slide. When producing your slides, the process will likely involve advice provided across each chapter of this section of the book. You'll determine the message, select the support, lay out the content, and repeat for the next slide.

Organize Supporting Information

Thalia was the senior legal counsel for a real estate investment firm with properties across North America and Europe. Her team had just completed due diligence on a potential portfolio acquisition—a set of mixed-use developments in Chicago—and the investment committee wanted her to summarize the legal risks on a single slide.

Thalia knew the key concerns: zoning irregularities on one property, an unresolved easement dispute on another, and an unfavorable clause buried in a property management agreement. She pulled together her findings, added short excerpts from the reports, flagged key clauses, and dropped everything into a bullet-heavy layout with multiple footnotes, boxes, and color-coded highlights.

When she walked the investment lead through the deck, he squinted at the screen and said, "This is everything but the kitchen sink."

Thalia had flagged the risks. But she put every piece of supporting information on the slide and didn't organize the information in any meaningful way. She delivered everything the investment committee asked for, just not in a way they could use.

Slides like Thalia's are common. The information is sound, but the organization undermines its impact. This chapter is about how to avoid that outcome. Before you learn how to organize your information effectively on a slide, let's look at common pitfalls that often get in the way.

Common Pitfalls

You can write an effective heading and develop excellent supporting information, but if your content isn't organized well on a slide, your audience might end up asking one or more of the following questions:

- Why is so much information crammed onto one slide?
- Why is this slide so hard to follow?
- What am I supposed to focus on first?

Slides that leave audiences feeling confused, overloaded, or distracted are ineffective. These reactions and feelings are common when a slide suffers from one of three pitfalls: too much information crammed onto a single slide, layouts that don't match the content, or poorly placed elements that create visual chaos.

- The *Everything but the Kitchen Sink* slide: Information is crammed onto one slide without determining how much is appropriate. This results in a cluttered "data dump" where nothing stands out. For example, a slide with 10 bullet points in small font, all presented as one large chunk that runs from margin to margin.
- The *One Size Fits None* slide: People choose a generic layout or one that doesn't match the content, resulting in some level of conscious or unconscious confusion for the audience. For example, a slide that includes three boxes when the content naturally fits into four.
- The *Where Do I Look* slide: Content is randomly placed on the slide, with no clear hierarchy or flow. The audience doesn't know where to start and is left feeling confused.

Each pitfall has something in common: They make slides more difficult to process. As you consider how to organize supporting information on a slide, aim to make the slide visually inviting and easy to navigate. A well-organized slide allows the audience to absorb information quickly and move through the content effortlessly.

How to Organize Supporting Information

Once you've identified the supporting information for the body of the content slide, organize it using five steps:

1. Identify which pieces of supporting information belong together.
2. Choose a layout that visually organizes the information.
3. Decide where each chunk belongs.
4. Make the structure clear at a glance.
5. Assess the information density of the slide.

If only slide design was as simple as checking off these five steps and declaring a slide complete. In reality, this is an iterative process. You might start by grouping your content, only to realize later that a different layout would make more sense. Or you might assess your slide's density and then realize that you need to go back and break out an overcrowded chunk. So, as you work through this process, remember that you'll likely have to revisit earlier steps.

Step 1: Identify Which Pieces of Supporting Information Belong Together

Now it's time to group your content into clear, meaningful chunks. A chunk is a self-contained unit of information that the audience perceives as distinct from everything else on the slide. It could be a block of text, a graphic, or a combination of both.

In the last chapter, you identified one or more graphics and considered whether additional text (beyond the heading) was needed to support your point. Now, you'll decide which elements—graphics and text—should be grouped together in distinct chunks.

You may recall from chapter 4 that a chunk refers to any information that your vision perceives as belonging to a group, separate from other groups around it. This step puts that definition into practice.

If you have only one graphic, the step is simple because you won't have any grouping to do. However, the more pieces of information you have, the more challenging it is to chunk. Let's discuss further why chunking is important and consider how many chunks are appropriate for one slide.

Why Chunks?

Imagine you're given a list of 10 random digits to memorize: 5558675309. No pattern, no grouping—just raw numbers. Most of us would struggle to hold them in our heads. But when the same numbers are arranged like a phone number—555-867-5309—suddenly, it's manageable. That's chunking in action.

Our brains aren't wired to process an endless stream of information. Working memory, the system our brain uses to temporarily hold and manipulate information, has strict limits. Cognitive scientist Alan Baddeley found that our working memory can only retain a few pieces of information at once before we start forgetting things.[1] That helps explain why grocery lists work better in categories and music is written in measures or bars.

The same principle applies to slides. When details are scattered across a slide with no clear organization, the audience has to work harder to process the information. But when we group related ideas together, we ease the burden and help the brain process and retain information more efficiently. Chunking makes content easier to follow and easier to remember.

Chunking also makes content more aesthetically pleasing by creating more organized slides. Studies in interface design and visual perception show that users judge layouts with clear groups and spacing as more attractive because they are easier to decode and less visually demanding.[2]

How Many Chunks?

Psychologist Nelson Cowan found that our working memory can hold about four distinct pieces of information at a time before its performance begins to decline.[3] That means when a slide presents more than four separate ideas, your audience has to work hard to retain those ideas—and if information isn't grouped meaningfully, your audience might check out altogether.

Effective slides typically have between one and four information chunks. At this point in the content-slide-creation process, the question you should ask yourself is this: How many distinct groups of information do I have to support my point?

Low-density slides tend to have fewer chunks, and high-density slides tend to have more chunks. The table offers general guidelines for how many chunks typically appear at each density level.

Information Chunks

	Information Chunks
Low Density	1–2
Medium Density	1–4
High Density	2–4

These are general guidelines, not hard-set rules. My guidance about chunks refers specifically to the body area of the slide—not to the heading, subheading, footer, or any design elements built into the slide master.

It's possible to have a low-density slide with three or four chunks of information (for example, a slide with three photographs). Recall our discussion from chapter 6 about how easily your audience can process different categories of graphics.

In contrast, a high-density slide with only one chunk is likely the result of poor design—imagine an all-text slide with dense paragraphs running from margin to margin.

Why Not Five Chunks?

By including too many chunks on a slide, you may exceed your audience's working memory capacity. If you find yourself with too many chunks, consider what information can be simplified, grouped, or moved to another slide:

- **Simplify the information.** Identify what is most critical for your audience to understand, and remove the rest. For a low-density deck, rather than putting everything on the slide, consider omitting extra information from the slide and reserving it for your speaking notes.
- **Group related chunks.** Look for logical relationships between chunks and combine them into a larger chunk. Use segment headings to label the grouped content.
- **Move information to another slide.** Assess which chunks are less essential to the main point of the current slide and transfer one or more chunks to a new slide. This may require adjusting the headline by reducing the scope of the claim and writing a new headline for the second slide—rather than repeating the same headline on both or using "Continued ..."

Is It Possible to Have Too Few Chunks?

Yes, it is possible to have too few chunks on a content slide. When a slide contains too little information, it may fail to fully support the headline. For example, a slide with one information chunk could require additional explanation for the presenter or risk misinterpretation. While minimalism is valuable, especially on a low-density slide, be sure to include enough information chunks to maintain clarity.

Wireframes

Once you've determined the number of chunks, consider how you will organize your content on the slide by sketching a quick wireframe of the slide.

Sketching a wireframe before adding content to a slide helps you

- Visualize the layout of the content without being distracted by design elements.
- Explore potential layout options before committing to a final design.
- Save time by identifying potential layout issues early.

Follow these five steps to sketch a wireframe for your slide:

1. **Sketch on paper.** Use a blank piece of paper, sticky notes, or index cards.
2. **Think in zones.** Focus on the content area in the middle of the slide (not the heading or footer area).
3. **Use simple shapes.** Draw simple boxes or lines to represent where text or graphics might go. This can be messy; it's not about being an artist.
4. **Work quickly.** Don't aim for perfection. If necessary, sketch two or three different layouts and pick the one that feels best.
5. **Reference existing slides.** Find inspiration in slides you or others have already created.

The visual on the next page shows how rough sketches can help you experiment with layout and structure before working in slide software.

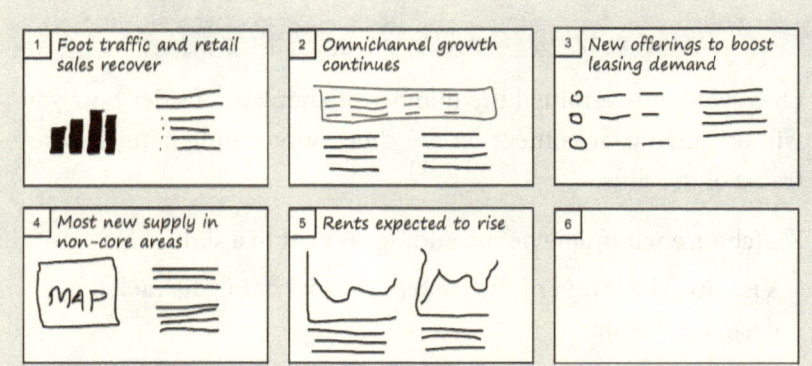

These rough sketches show how key messages and supporting content might be arranged on individual slides. Wireframes like these help presenters visualize content flow, explore layout options, and identify potential design issues early—before committing time to slide formatting or design.

Step 2: Choose a Layout that Visually Organizes the Information

Once you've chunked your supporting content and, as a result, determined how many chunks you are working with, you will be ready to choose a layout to organize the information. Layouts are a way to make chunking visible to the audience, so they intuitively process the information the way you intend. Each placeholder in a layout can serve as the home for the chunk of information you identified in Step 1.

It turns out that a graphic designer has figured out that you can organize the body of a slide 892 different ways.[4] This abundance of options might explain the paralysis many people feel when attempting to organize elements effectively on a slide.

I have good news: My research has revealed that the most effective layouts employ some version of one of three basic layouts—whole, half, or thirds. (These names refer to the relative width of chunks on a slide.)

At this stage in the process, you should ask yourself what layout best fits the number and type of chunks you've identified.

The illustration below shows these three core layouts. They serve as the foundation for many other layouts.

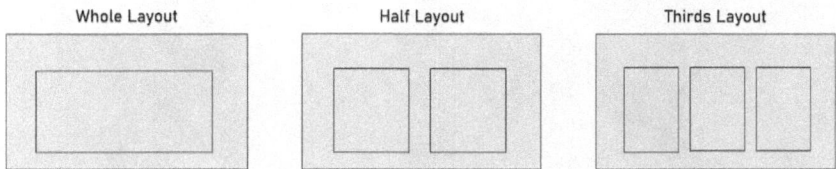

Here you can see the core layouts that most slides build on. These layout patterns should help you visually organize chunks of information to match the quantity and type of content you plan to include on content slides.

Whole layout: Use the whole-slide body layout when you have a large graphic to display with limited to no textual elaboration. The graphic should take up most of the slide beneath the heading. The example on the next page shows how a whole layout can emphasize a single, dominant chunk of information.

This slide uses most of the content area to highlight a single chart and message, making the point visually clear and immediately scannable. Whole layouts are most effective when you have one dominant chunk of information.

Half layout: Use the half-slide body layout when you have two chunks of information. The most common approach is to present the chunks side by side (left to right). However, on some occasions you can use the half layout to stack two chunks (top/down).

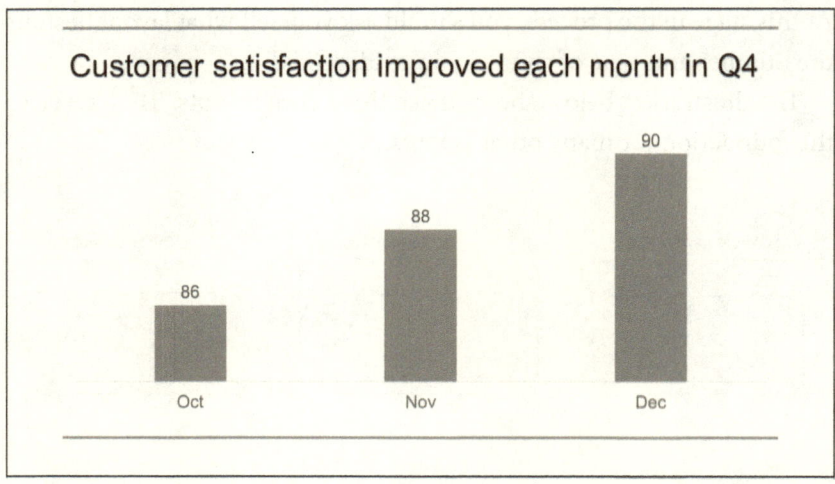

The downside of stacking is that if you're using explanatory text, it can run from margin to margin—making it harder for your audience to process. This has to do with how the eye moves across the slide, a topic covered in more detail later in this chapter. The example that follows uses a side-by-side layout, which helps prevent that issue.

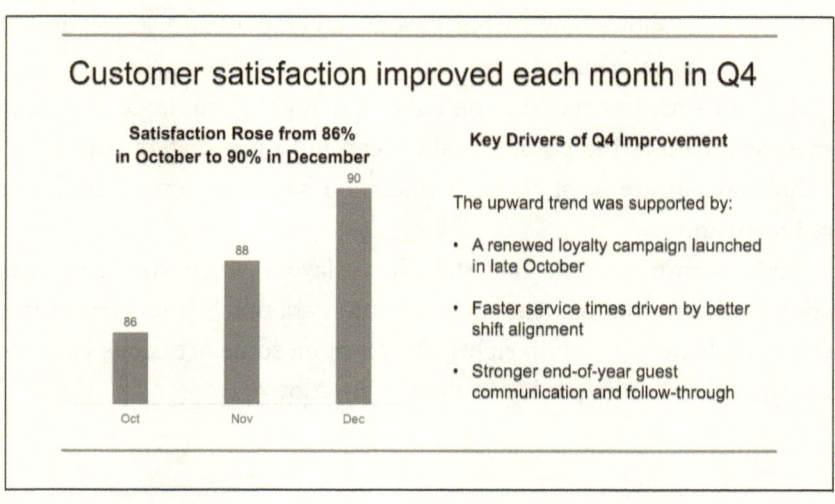

The medium-density slide uses two equally weighted content areas: a graphic on the left and brief explanatory text on the right. This side-by-side layout helps keep the content skimmable.

The most common variation of the half layout is to break the halves into half—creating four chunks of equal size. Consider whether you want your audience to view the chunks top down or left to right (or it might not matter). The next example shows a two-by-two structure that presents four interrelated ideas with supporting detail.

This high-density slide uses a combination of segment headings and bulleted lists to maintain readability, even with a larger amount of text.

Thirds layout: Use the thirds-slide body layout when you have two or three chunks of information. For three chunks, divide the slide into three equal-width columns arranged from left to right, as seen in the example on the next page.

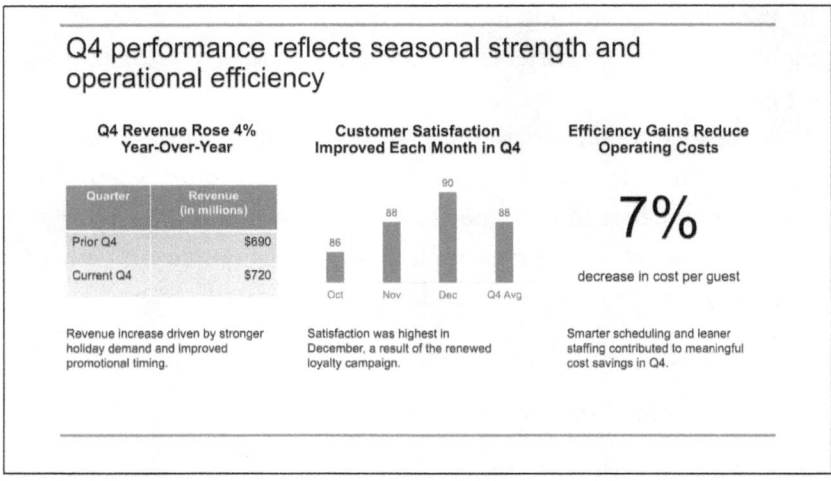

This layout presents three insights side by side, each with a segment heading, graphic, and supporting explanation. Equal-width columns make this medium-density slide visually balanced.

For two chunks, the thirds layout can be adapted into an asymmetric split—with one chunk taking up two-thirds of the slide and the other occupying one-third. The larger chunk can appear on either the left or the right, depending on what you want to emphasize. While it's possible to stack content vertically using thirds, the layout is rarely effective.

The thirds layout also offers several variations:

- Divide the two-thirds section into two horizontal parts while keeping the one-third section intact, creating three chunks overall.

- Split both sections (two-thirds and one-third) horizontally, resulting in four total chunks.

- Split the equal-thirds layout in half horizontally, producing a six-part layout.[5]

The following graphic illustrates a two-thirds/one third layout, with the larger section used for a graphic and the smaller section for explanatory text.

This medium-density variation emphasizes the importance of the chart while allowing room for supporting detail on the side. The thirds layout is ideal for highlighting a key data story with moderate textual elaboration.

These layouts are a great place to start but are by no means your only options. Many variations within these three layouts are possible. For example, the thirds layout could include two charts in the larger two-thirds part of the slide and one chunk of explanatory text in the one-third area of the slide.

Step 3: Decide Where Each Chunk Belongs

Ideally, as you are considering which layout is best, you should be thinking about not only which chunks you are working with, but also where you could place them. As you decide, ask yourself: What do I want my audience to see first, second, and so on? To answer that question, you need to anticipate how your audience will look at your slide and make design choices to guide them through it in a way that makes the most sense for your message.

Establish a Clear Visual Hierarchy

Beyond the slide heading (and possible subheading), consider where you want your readers to look first, and design the body of the content slide to create a natural flow for the readers' eyes. You might base your choices on the logical reading path, the relative importance of each chunk, or how the chunks relate to one another.

- **Flow:** Does the placement of each chunk create a logical flow that's easy for the audience to follow?
- **Importance:** What's the most important piece of information, and where should it go for maximum impact?
- **Relationships:** How can you organize related chunks to make connections clear to the audience?

Let's begin with some foundational assumptions about how business audiences around the world read English-language documents.

- People tend to read English left to right and top down.
- Aligned elements create a visual path that helps guide the audience.
- Larger elements will attract more attention than smaller elements.
- Brighter colors will usually attract more attention than muted colors.
- Elements closer to each other are more related than items further way.
- White space separates distinct ideas and helps reduce cognitive load.

When one or more chunks are a graphic and one or more chunks are explanatory text, you need to consider whether you want the audience to see the graphic first or text first:

- **Graphic first:** Present the graphic toward the top and left side of the slide (below the headline and sub-headline) if you believe the audience can process the graphic without seeing the explanatory text first. Then place explanatory text beneath or to the right of the graphic. Consider this approach when you create medium-density decks.

- **Text first:** If you feel the audience needs context before they can process the graphic, place the explanatory text toward the top and left side of the slide (below the headline and sub-headline). Then place the graphic beneath or to the right of the text. This approach may be most common in high-density decks that will be read rather than presented.

As you decide, keep in mind that the headline (and possibly the sub-headline) may sufficiently set up the graphic (i.e., the graphic can be the first thing the audience sees in the slide body). As discussed in the previous chapter, strong segment headings for chunks can reduce the need for explanatory text as well.

Placing your chunks is only part of the process. You also need to think about how the content within each one is presented.

Try This with AI

Evaluate slide hierarchy. *Prompt:* "This slide has multiple elements: [describe content]. Can you help me decide how to lay them out to make the hierarchy visually clear?"

Lay Out the Text

Even experienced slide designers can find it challenging to lay out text effectively. Most of us learned to write using word processing software, where text runs continuously from margin to margin. In that context, our main decision is simply when to insert a paragraph break.

But laying out text on a slide requires a different approach. You should try to avoid using a wall of text. In the core layouts presented in this chapter, chunks don't run from margin to margin—and that's intentional. Slide body text should not span the full width of a slide.

The core layouts help prevent margin-to-margin text, which is typical in a text-dominant document like letters and memos but doesn't translate well to slides. The following example shows what happens when paragraphs run margin to margin, even when the content is logically grouped.

Leaner staffing lowered cost per guest

Leaner staffing model

Reducing baseline staffing during nonpeak hours helped control labor costs without compromising service. Instead of staffing based on fixed coverage templates, managers used historical demand patterns to build more flexible rosters. For example, some locations shifted from static morning and evening shifts to staggered start times, better aligning hours worked with guest volume. These changes also made scheduling more adaptable in response to real-time fluctuations. As one of our managers noted, "The goal isn't fewer people—it's the right people, at the right time."

Cross-trained employees

Empowering employees to take on multiple responsibilities enabled greater operational agility. For instance, front-desk staff trained to assist with concierge tasks and food runners who could support housekeeping during turnover periods made it easier to maintain service quality without additional head count. Cross-training also helped reduce idle time by allowing employees to pivot based on guest flow and priority needs. A recent industry survey found that 68% of operators who cross-trained reported improvements in shift productivity.

Optimized resource allocation

Aligning labor, supplies, and services more closely with actual demand led to a measurable drop in cost per guest. Teams used simple forecasting tools—sometimes just spreadsheets based on prior-year trends—to adjust staffing levels and reduce waste. For example, instead of pre-staging full amenities on all floors, supply distribution was adjusted dynamically based on room occupancy. This shift not only cut costs but also improved inventory management across departments.

Although this slide has three distinct chunks, the margin-to-margin layout makes it difficult to scan.

As you lay out slide content, think like a magazine designer. Except for slide headings and subheadings, most text and graphic elements should span no more than two-thirds of the slide's width.

The goal is to limit the number of eye sweeps—the instances when your audience's eyes move from the left margin to the right. Full-width text creates long, horizontal eye sweeps, while narrow columns of text force too many short return sweeps.

Instead, aim for a column width that is neither too wide nor too narrow. The following example shows three commonly effective text widths for slides.

Lorem ipsum dolor sit amet consectetur temo metus Bibendum elit.
|-------------------------- 2/3 width --------------------------|

Quisque faucibus ex sapien vitae pellensque sem.
|---------------- 1/2 width -----------------|

Ad litora torquent per conubia vel.
|--------- 1/3 width ----------|

This graphic illustrates three appropriate text widths, ranging from one-third to two-thirds of the slide. When using body text, consider limiting the line length to improve scanning and comprehension.

To help you consider how to divide the slide, display any gridlines or guides that may be available. (In PowerPoint, you will find this feature under the "View" tab.) The examples that follow show how to apply a one-third layout to organize multiple chunks of text, either side by side or stacked vertically.

One-third layout (three columns): Place a heading at the top of each column. Use this layout when textual elaboration for each column is relatively brief, as shown in the next example.

This layout places headings at the top of each column, making it ideal for summarizing multiple themes or categories side by side.

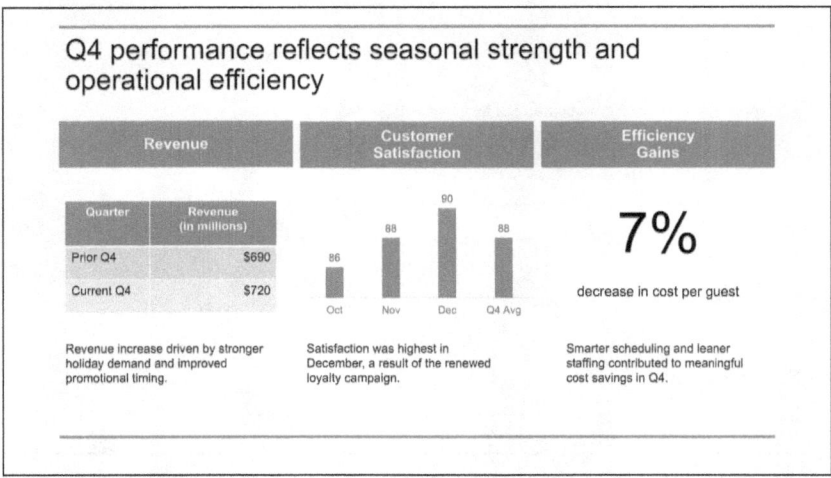

One-third layout (three rows): Place a heading to the left of each row. Use this layout when textual elaboration for each row is lengthy, as shown in the example below.

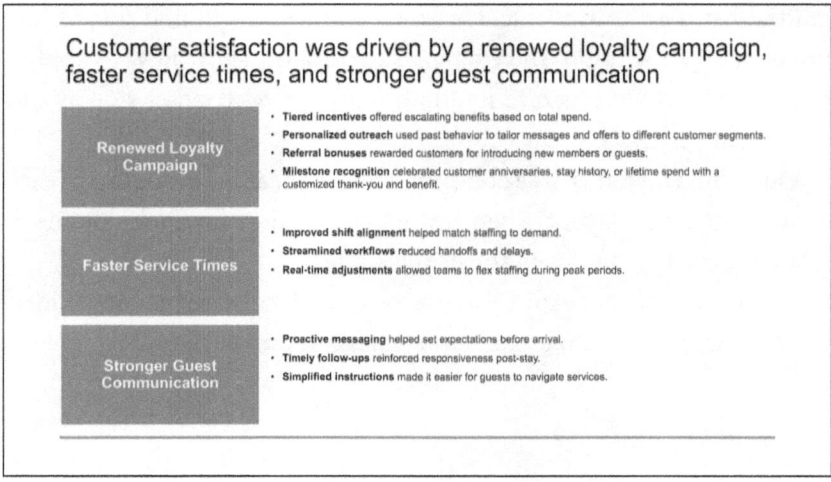

This layout places headings to the left of each row, allowing more space for detailed explanations. It's best suited for slides where each category or idea requires several lines of elaboration.

Place Graphics Within Chunks

You need to give each graphic enough space to function effectively. One of the most common mistakes in slide design is squeezing graphics into chunks that are too tight. If a graphic is too small, your audience may struggle to interpret it. A large, well-positioned graphic signals importance and often becomes the focal point of the slide.

In low-density decks, graphics often occupy their own chunk entirely. As slide density increases, you may pair a graphic with explanatory text inside the same chunk.

Many graphics also benefit from brief textual support. Labels, captions, and brief explanations can help clarify what the audience is looking at and why it matters. When you combine a graphic with text in the same chunk, be sure their relationship is visually clear. Your audience should see at a glance how the elements connect.

Step 4: Make the Structure Clear at a Glance

When someone looks at your slide, their brain instantly starts organizing the information. Before they consciously process the content, they instinctively group elements based on visual cues. If you understand how this works, you can design slides that are easier for your audience to navigate.

Gestalt theory, a field of psychology that explores how humans perceive patterns, explains that our brains don't process information one item at a time. Instead, we look for structure and relationships. Whether you're scanning a restaurant menu or scrolling through your social media feed, your brain is constantly grouping, organizing, and prioritizing what you see. This theory suggests that we naturally group information based on proximity, similarity, connection, and enclosure.[6]

You can use these four principles to help your audience recognize how information is grouped on your slides.

- **Proximity:** Our brains group elements based on how close they are to each other—often before noticing color, lines, or shapes.

To apply this principle, place related content close together so your audience sees it as a single chunk. Keep segment headings directly above the content they introduce, and position explanatory text near the corresponding graphics. If related elements are too far apart, your audience might not realize they belong together.

- **Similarity:** Once we see proximity, we look for patterns. Elements that share a common color, shape, or style naturally feel related. You can group related information by maintaining a consistent color, shape, and alignment for elements that belong in the same chunk. If two elements serve the same function, signal that connection through design choices.

- **Connectedness:** When proximity or similarity isn't enough to show relationships, you can use visual cues to make connections clear. You can add lines, arrows, or other visual connectors to chunk elements. Segment headings can also reinforce connectedness by labeling groups of related content. Connectedness is especially useful when content is visually separated but conceptually linked.

- **Enclosure:** When you want to ensure your audience views a set of ideas as a single chunk, place them inside a box, colored background, or shaded area. These methods are among the strongest ways to signal grouping—but use them selectively. Enclosure can make a slide feel visually heavy, and using large blocks of light text on a dark background can strain your audience's eyes. When possible, try applying the principles of proximity, similarity, or connectedness first.

Without these principles, your audience is less likely to recognize related content as a single chunk. And while these four design principles help your audience group information, it's just as important to prevent them from grouping things that don't belong together.

Separation techniques help make chunks distinct from one another. Effective separation prevents the audience from mistakenly connecting unrelated pieces of information.

- **White space**: More space between elements weakens their connection, making it easier for the audience to distinguish separate chunks.

- **Dividing lines**: A thin horizontal or vertical line can create a clear boundary between chunks of content.

- **Misalignment**: Elements that don't align are less likely to be perceived as related. (Although, I advocate for aligning chunks with other chunks.)

By combining chunking techniques with separation strategies, you create slides that are both structured and intuitive.

Step 5: Assess the Information Density of the Slide

In the planning stage, you identified the target level of information density for the deck. Now is the time to check whether each slide aligns with your goal. The point isn't to reduce density for its own sake. Instead, your aim is to ensure that most slides land close to your intended density target. Some variation is fine.

To help guide this assessment, the table below combines two key dimensions of slide density: word count and information chunks. The ranges are based on insights from communication practitioners and analysis of workplace slide decks.[7]

Information Density Guidelines

	Low Density	Medium Density	High Density
Word Count	< 50	50–100	100–250
Information Chunks	1–2	1–4	2–4

These figures are intended to help you assess—not dictate—your slide's density. If a slide falls outside these ranges, it's worth asking: Is the level of density intentional? Does the slide match the audience's needs and the purpose of the deck? The goal is to help you make the slide as effective as possible, not to lock you into a formula.

Making Adjustments Based on Your Density Check

As a result of your assessment, you will reach one of three possible outcomes:

1. **The information density is just right.** If the information density matches what you planned for, move on to your next content slide.

2. **The information density is too low.** If the slide has too few information chunks or if the word count is too low, it may be underdeveloped. That said, audiences are generally more forgiving of low-density slides than overly dense ones. So, you may not need to adjust it. But before moving on, consider whether anything important is missing. One way to test this is to show the slide to a colleague and ask if any additional information on the slide could help them more easily understand your point.

3. **The information density is too high.** If the slide includes too many information chunks or the word count is too high, it may present more information than your audience can reasonably absorb.

    a. Start by looking for ways to reduce the word count—tighten your language and eliminate anything that isn't essential.

    b. Consider whether you can remove an entire chunk without weakening the overall message.

    c. If trimming both the words and the chunks still doesn't bring the density to recommended ranges, consider splitting the content into two or more slides. To make this work, you'll need to narrow the scope of the heading so that each slide requires less supporting information.

d. If you need to present a high-density slide live, consider using builds to control how the information appears. Reveal one chunk at a time to help your audience follow along. Use simple entrance animations and avoid unnecessary motion that could distract from your message.

Guiding Principles by Density Level

Here's some additional guidance about how to assess the information density of your content slides, focusing on white space, graphic size, text size, the role of headings, reading time, and word count.

Low Density

Low-density slides should prioritize graphics over text to support live presentations. The presenter should be the main focus, and the slides should serve as visual support, not a script. These slides should have the most white space—giving the content room to breathe and enabling audience to process information quickly.

To design low-density slides that support live delivery, focus on these principles:

- **White space**: Essential. Keep the slide visually clean.
- **Graphics**: Larger. A well-chosen graphic can stand alone without supporting text, allowing the presenter to explain it in real time.
- **Body text size**: Larger than medium- or high-density deck. Body text, if used, should be big enough to read from the back of the room—typically 20 points or more.
- **Role of headings**: Topic or question headings can work well, since the presenter provides the key points orally.
- **Reading time**: The slide should pass Nancy Duarte's "glance test"—where an audience should be able to grasp the slide's message in about three seconds.
- **Word count**: Duarte also states that if a slide has more than 50 words, it risks becoming a teleprompter instead of a visual aid.[8]

Medium Density

Medium-density slides should balance graphics and text, making them versatile enough to support both live presentations and situations where the deck will be reviewed independently—such as a pre-read or leave-behind. As you assess your slides, ask yourself two questions: Will a live audience be able to follow this slide quickly while I speak? Will a reader, without me there, understand the main point? If the answer to either question is no, the slide likely needs adjustment—either by reducing the amount of text or adding more supporting details.

A well-designed medium-density slide typically reflects the following characteristics:

- **White space:** Moderate. More content than low-density slides, but white space is used between chunks.

- **Graphics:** Typically smaller than low-density-decks, as they often share space with supporting text.

- **Body text size:** Typically smaller than low-density decks and larger than high-density decks (i.e., 14 to 19 points).

- **Role of headings:** When you create a deck that needs to serve dual purposes, use a headline to surface your main point. A graphic stands a much better chance of standing alone when introduced by a strong headline.

  - ▸ **Live headline**: New pricing increased conversions by 20%

  - ▸ **Dual-purpose headline**: New pricing model led to a 20% increase in conversions over six months

- **Reading time:** The slide should be easy to process, but it may take slightly longer than a low-density slide. If you know your audience will need to read the deck later, rather than overloading individual slides, create more slides.

- **Word count:** Between 50 and 100 words is typically sufficient for a deck that must serve dual purposes.

High Density

High-density slides are content rich and best suited for situations where the slide deck will be read as a document. Design each slide to make stand-alone sense. Because your readers may not have the opportunity to converse with you about the deck, each slide must convey and fully support a key idea.

Effective high-density slides often share the following design features:

- **White space:** Low. Less space between information chunks.
- **Graphics:** Smaller than in other deck types.
- **Body text size:** Smaller than in low- and medium-density slides, similar to what you would use in a traditional report (i.e., 10 to 12 points).
- **Role of headings:** Use headlines to provide the main point of the slide. Use sub-headlines to increase comprehension.
- **Reading time:** High-density slides take longer to read but should still be designed for scanning.
- **Word count:** When preparing what Nancy Duarte calls a *SlideDoc*, she suggests anywhere between 100 to 250 words per slide is appropriate. If you start to exceed 250 words on one slide, consider breaking the content into two (or more) slides.

If you are preparing a stand-alone deck—one that your audience will read without you presenting—your graphics will likely need textual elaboration. This added context helps ensure that the message is interpreted the way you intend. In a live presentation, you can explain the meaning of the graphic out loud. In a stand-alone deck, the text must do that work for you.

Audiences who are more knowledgeable—or more motivated to explore material in depth—can typically handle higher-information-density slides. In contrast, less knowledgeable or less motivated audiences may benefit from slides with lower density.

A well-designed slide respects the audience's intelligence by presenting information clearly using visual hierarchy, grouping, and alignment to make relationships and priorities intuitive. A knowledgeable and motivated audience may be able to process high-density slides more easily than a less knowledgeable or less motivated one. For example, a slide showing intricate financial data may be appropriate when presenting to institutional investors who are accustomed to examining detailed charts and models. But that same slide might include too much information for a nonprofit board or executive team who need a clear summary of what the data means.

Chapter 7 Takeaways

- When a slide feels confusing, cluttered, or directionless, it likely suffers from too much information, a mismatched layout, or chaotic placement.
- Group related content into meaningful chunks—typically one to four per slide.
- Choose a layout that reflects the number and nature of your chunks (e.g., whole, half, thirds).
- Organize chunks by flow, importance, or relationship—and design the slide to reflect that hierarchy.
- Apply Gestalt principles like proximity, similarity, connectedness, and enclosure to make structure clear at a glance.
- Evaluate whether the slide's information density matches your deck's intended purpose and your audience's needs.

Once you've grouped your content, chosen a layout, and positioned your elements, your slides are ready—but not quite finished. The next step is to polish your deck, so it functions as cohesive whole. In Part III, you'll learn how to design special-purpose slides, fine-tune individual content slides, and strengthen the story that ties your deck together.

POLISHING YOUR SLIDE DECKS

Polishing your slide deck is the last step in the slide deck creation process. It's the step where you can turn a good deck into a memorable one. Yet many communicators skip this step when deadlines approach. That's why effective time management is essential. You need enough time not only to craft your slide content, but also to refine it. And, if you are presenting or facilitating, you'll need time to rehearse with your slides as well.

The little details can make a big difference.

Polishing tasks, such as creating special-purpose slides, refining the details within each slide, and ensuring consistency across the entire deck, will improve the clarity, cohesion, and professionalism of your slide deck. In this section, we'll explore these finishing steps in three chapters:

- **Chapter 8: Create Special-Purpose Slides**—Learn how to design agenda slides, section dividers, and other slides that serve a unique role in guiding your audience through your deck.

- **Chapter 9: Fine-Tune Within Each Slide**—Understand techniques to refine individual slides for improved clarity and impact.

- **Chapter 10: Strengthen the Story Across the Deck**—Improve consistency throughout your entire slide deck.

With proper planning you'll have sufficient time to polish your deck. As you review your deck, ask yourself, What's unclear?

Create Special-Purpose Slides

Avery had spent months working on the new performance evaluation process. As director of human resources at a midsized manufacturing company, he knew this change wouldn't be easy. The old system was outdated and inconsistent. His team had piloted a new set of performance standards, gathered feedback, and refined the approach. Now, it was time to roll it out across the company.

Avery's slide deck was packed with useful information. It walked through the problems with the old process, detailed the new evaluation criteria, showed example scorecards, and laid out an implementation timeline. He delivered the presentation in a department head meeting, walking through the slides with confidence.

But when he wrapped up, the questions surprised him.

"Are we being asked for input, or is this final?"

"Can we see a summary of what's changing?"

"What are the next steps after this meeting?"

Avery realized the issue wasn't with the content itself. It was the lack of framing. Without slides to preview, summarize, or close the presentation, his audience had no clear sense of where they were or what to do next. There was no agenda slide at the start, no executive summary to preview the key changes, and no closing slide to reinforce what came next. The body of the deck was strong, but it was missing the important structural slides that help a deck function as an effective communication tool.

———————————— ■ ————————————

When time is short or content is complex, it's easy to overlook the slides that guide your audience through the experience: the title slide, the executive summary, the agenda or table of contents, the section dividers, and the closing. But these special-purpose slides are what help your audience stay oriented, grasp the big picture, and act on what they've learned.

This chapter explores how to create and refine those essential slides.

Special-purpose slides guide the audience through the deck's structure and highlight its key components. These slides serve as navigational aids, setting the stage for the deck, summarizing key points, or delineating major sections.

Although I suggest that you create special-purpose slides as one of your polishing activities, you can start with your special-purpose slides or your content slides—or move back and forth between the two.

If you choose to create special-purpose slides before your content slides, be sure to revisit and revise your special-purpose slides before sharing your deck. For example, although you may prepare your table of contents or agenda and executive summary slides first, it's usually best to finalize those slides after your content slides are complete.

Title Slide

A title slide typically includes the title of the slide deck, information about the author, and the date. Some title slides will also identify the report's target audience.

- **Deck title:** Provide audiences with enough information so that they can confidently predict what they will learn if they make their way through the entire deck. Many writers find it helpful to begin the title with one of these three structures:
  - ▸ **Verb phrase**: Increasing Engagement via Personalized Social Media Campaigns

- ▸ **Question**: How Can We Increase Engagement via Personalized Social Media Campaigns?
- ▸ **Noun phrase + subtitle**: Personalized Social Media Campaigns: A Great Way to Increase Engagement
- **Author:** In addition to identifying the author's name and title, you may consider adding company affiliations when you prepare a deck for an external audience.
- **Audience:** Identify the primary audience members by name, title, and company (for example, "Prepared for the Board of Directors, Acme Corporation.").
- **Date:** Because some slide decks have long shelf lives, including a date is especially helpful for audiences who may review the deck at a later date. To minimize ambiguity, spell out the month, followed by the day and year in numerical format.
- **Footer information:** If applicable, include an unobtrusive text box toward the bottom of the slide with a legal notice, copyright statement, and/or administrative information (like version control numbers).

Executive Summary

Consider including an executive summary, especially for a deck that will at some point need to make stand-alone sense. An executive summary provides a synopsis: a reduced version of your slide-deck content.

Why Include an Executive Summary?

Regardless of the deck's length, executives want to find the most important information quickly. An effective executive summary enables the audience to discern the main ideas and determine whether to continue listening or reading. A well-designed executive summary lets your audience distill the key information at a glance, read selectively (and zoom in where appropriate), and make decisions—without necessarily reading the entire document.

Consulting firms call this approach *Answer First*. Military communicators call it *BLUF—Bottom Line Up Front*. The labels differ, but they have the same premise: Demonstrate respect for your audience's time by surfacing your highest-level points at the start of the deck.

What Belongs on the Slide?

Think of an executive summary as a miniature, stand-alone version of the whole deck. Consider including the words *Executive Summary* in the heading location and answer the governing question in the sub-headline. To be effective, the slide should meet four quality tests, as shown in the following table.

Executive Summary Quality Test

Quality Test	Practical Meaning for a Slide
Self-sufficient	Audience understands your message without seeing another slide.
Selectively redundant	Key facts and graphics reappear later for detail seekers.
Proportional in length	Usually one slide for a brief deck; up to 5–10% of total slides in a longer deck.
High skim value	Consider including a topic heading, message sub-headline; avoid margin-to-margin text; organize into 3 or 4 chunks.

As You Prepare an Executive Summary, What Process Should You Follow?

Choose the approach that fits your working style and deadline:

A. Answer the Governing Question

    1. Identify the single question the deck must answer.

    2. Draft a one-sentence answer as your sub-headline.

    3. Surface your main points to support the conclusion.

Elevator Test: Image that you have 60 seconds in an elevator with your audience. What would you say to convey your main point? Write that out, then distill it into a concise sub-headline and supporting points. Use a layout that's visually inviting and easy to skim—so your audience can grasp the message quickly.

B. Reduce-Then-Stack

1. Draft the content slides first.

2. Reduce each section to one sentence and one key graphic.

3. Stack those micro-sections into a single slide.

4. Make sure the summary flows clearly from one point to the next.

Try This with AI

Generate an executive summary. *Prompt:* "Based on the main message and supporting points in this deck, can you draft the text for a one-slide executive summary?"

Executive Summary Checklist

An effective executive summary provides readers with a high-level overview:

- Write the executive summary after you prepare the content slides. (Summarize the main recommendations and conclusions that unfold in the body.)
- Identify which points are essential to your synopsis—by checking major sections (section divider slides) and headlines.
- Consider including essential evidence or data points.
- Write in full sentences (and paragraphs), rather than fragments.
- Limit yourself to information found on content slides (i.e., don't include new information).

- Edit the final draft for clarity and coherence.

- Design the summary to be visually inviting. Executive summaries tend to include text, but that doesn't mean you should forget what you've learned about laying out information on a slide. Remember to avoid wall-to-wall text and instead use chunks to organize content on a slide. Although tables, charts, and diagrams may be suitable for the report body, they are less common in an executive summary.

- If you decide to include an executive summary, place it immediately after the title slide (or as soon as you can), rather than after other front-end matter (like the table of contents).

A crisp executive summary signals respect for your audience. In some cases, the executive summary can determine whether the rest of your work gets read at all.

Agenda Slide (Table of Contents Slide)

When you provide a preview of your slide deck's structure, you help your audience know what to expect. This preview typically takes the form of an agenda slide or a table of contents (TOC) slide.

Both list the main topics or sections of your deck, but they differ slightly in format and use. An agenda slide is generally used in decks that will be presented live and typically omits slide numbers. A table of contents slide, more common in decks that are meant to be read, usually includes slide numbers or page references to help readers navigate the document.

The Best Practices for Both Slides Are Similar

The first decision to make when creating these types of special-purpose slides is to decide whether you will list the topics or points that follow in the slide deck. This decision is like the decision you must make when writing a content-slide heading (discussed in chapter 5).

Choose a *list of topics* when you want to introduce the structure without revealing your conclusions. This approach works well when

- Your audience doesn't need (or want) specific details upfront.
- You want to orient your audience without overloading them with information.
- You want the flexibility to adapt when presenting in a collaborative setting or discussion-oriented meeting.

A *list of points* works best when your goal is to signal conclusions or guide interpretation, such as when

- Your audience wants a preview of your main points upfront.
- You want to set clear expectations of the structure to help your audience follow along.
- You want to reassure the audience that you will be addressing their concerns.

As with most decisions you'll make when creating slide decks, you should base your decision not on what you prefer, but on what your audience needs.

Where people often go wrong: They operate under the assumption that they should keep their audience in suspense. In an attempt to control the narrative, they worry about revealing too much information up front.

For example, they might list generic topics:

- Problem
- Causes
- Opportunity
- Recommendation

Although these topics preview the structure of the deck, they don't provide enough detail about the content unless verbally supported with details. You can convert the topics listed above to points:

- Profit Margins Are Falling
- Inefficiencies Are Driving Costs Higher

- Operational Improvements Offer Cost Savings
- Supply Chain Processes Can Boost Profitability

The first approach forecasts the structure, while the second approach forecasts the structure and the content. Another option is to combine these two approaches (e.g., Problem: Profit Margins Are Falling).

Match Agenda Phrasing to Section-Divider Phrasing

Regardless of the approach you take to provide your audience with a preview of the deck contents, the phrasing you use in your agenda slide or table of contents slide should match the phrasing in the rest of the slide deck.

For example, if you've included section-divider slides to help organize the deck, you can simply copy and paste the titles of the section-divider slides on the agenda or TOC slide.

If you haven't organized your deck with section-divider slides, you may find it more challenging to decide what to include on your agenda slide. Some slide-deck creators make the incorrect assumption that they should list the headings from every content slide in their deck. That's like listing every page of a book in its table of contents. Unless the slide deck only includes a limited number of slides, a list of every content slide can make the agenda feel cluttered and difficult to process.

Use Grammatically Parallel Phrasing for Major Sections, as Well as Each Set of Subsections

Keep the grammatical structure consistent. You can do this by matching the type of word used to begin each phrase (e.g., match nouns with nouns and verbs with verbs). You should also be sure verb phrases are in the same tense and that noun phrases match in number (i.e., singular or plural).

In the following example, you'll see that major sections (labeled with numbers) all begin with verbs, and all the subsections (labeled with letters) begin with nouns.

1. Define the Opportunity
   a. Market Size
   b. Gap Analysis
   c. Regulatory Map
2. Validate Demand
   a. Customer Survey Findings
   b. Interview Insights
   c. Usage Data Analysis
3. Select the Winning Strategy
   a. Option Comparison
   b. ROI Model
   c. Assumption Stress Test
4. Commit to Action
   a. Owner Assignment
   b. Milestone Schedule
   c. Metric Tracking Plan

All major sections should share one grammatical pattern, and each set of subsections should share one grammatical pattern. The two sets of sections don't need to mirror each other—a verb-based heading can comfortably sit above noun-based bullets—as long as every item within each level is written in the same style. In short, help readers by making each line echo its peers, not its parent.

Create an Agenda or Table of Contents Slide

Now that you understand the shared best practices for agenda and table of contents slides, let's walk though guidance specific to each type.

Agenda slide: Agenda slides are also referred to as *road map* or *preview* slides because, when used during a live presentation, they display the main structure of the presentation while the speaker provides an oral preview.

The agenda should emphasize the main topics or points of the body of the presentation and generally omit references to other special-purpose slides: introduction, agenda, conclusion, and Q&A slides. The agenda typically should appear soon, but not necessarily immediately, after your title slide. For example, when presenting to a live audience, you might use one or more slides at the start to set the stage for your presentation before providing a road map of the structure and content.

You can take at least one of three possible approaches for the heading of an agenda slide:

1. Use the word *Agenda* in the heading.
2. Use the word *Agenda* in the heading and make a point in the sub-headline.
3. Make a point in the heading (and omit the word *Agenda*).

Agenda items can be presented vertically (top down) or horizontally (left to right). The top-down approach works well for combining topics and points, as in the example below.

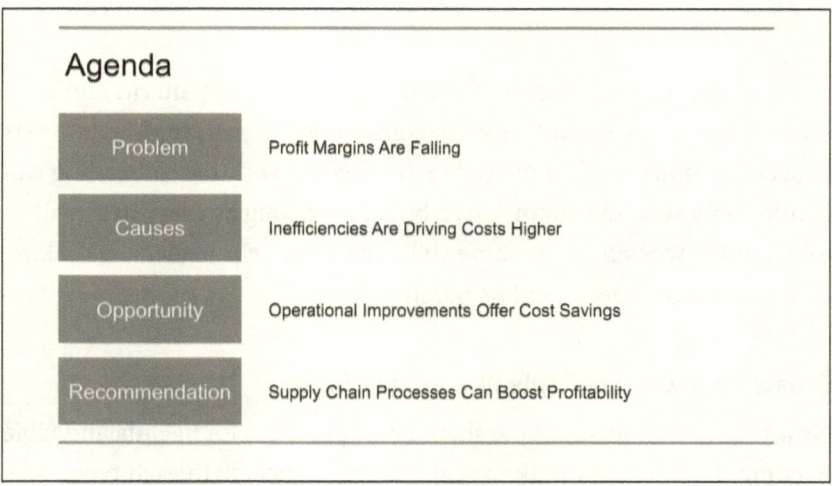

This slide presents the agenda in a top-down sequence, linking high-level topics (Problem, Causes, Opportunity, Recommendation) with concise points. The format previews the storyline and gives the audience a clear road map for the presentation.

Alternatively, a left-to-right agenda often works best when previewing topics only, as shown below.

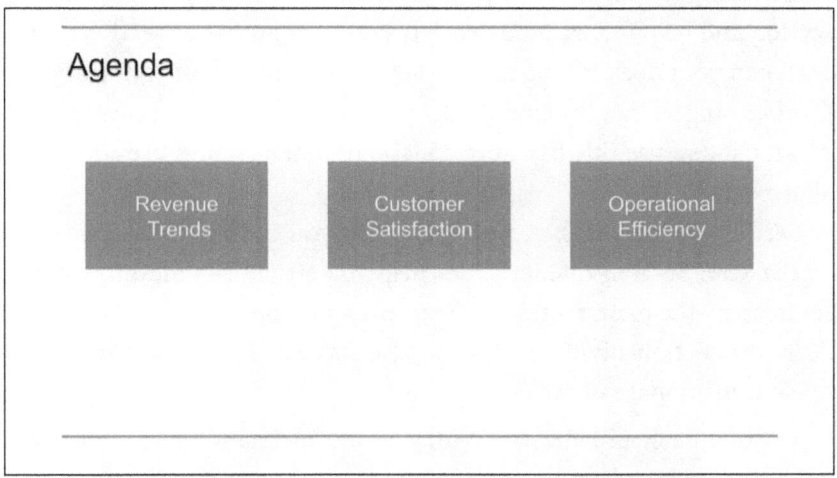

This slide previews the structure of a performance update using three high-level topics. Presented from left to right, the layout reflects the natural flow of the presentation without revealing the specific points. This approach works well when the details are introduced gradually or when the goal is to maintain flexibility in delivery.

Table of contents slide: A table of contents slide allows readers to find content quickly and easily by including slide numbers.

To prepare an effective table of contents, follow these tips:

- List the main topics from the slide deck body, as well as other deck elements, including appendices.
- For longer decks, consider identifying not only main sections but also subsections.
- Identify the executive summary (if it follows the table of contents)—but not the title slide.
- Place the table of contents before or after the executive summary.

Section-Divider Slides

Section-divider slides mark the transition between major parts of a slide deck. These low-density slides typically display the title of the upcoming section and help forecast the deck's overall structure. Use section dividers when your deck is long or complex—especially when your audience is processing a large amount of information. For the text on each of your divider slides, use title case, use consistent font size, and use consistent alignment.

Section-divider slides can be helpful for you and your audience.

For you: Section-divider slides help you structure (and more easily remember) the main sections of your presentation. When you present a deck, the section-divider slides can also serve as a reminder for you to make transitional statements:

- **Look back and ahead:** "With a clear understanding of inefficiencies raising costs, we can now explore the operational improvements that can help address these challenges."

- **Look ahead:** "Let's turn our attention to how streamlining supply chain processes can drive greater profitability."

For your audience: Section-divider slides help your audience follow your presentation more easily. Because people's minds wander, a divider slide can provide just enough change to recapture their attention and allow them to mentally refocus on your presentation and anticipate what comes next.

For you and your audience: Section-divider slides also provide you and your audience with a brief pause. You can use this pause to check in with your audience or engage them more broadly with the content. A check-in might involve gauging their understanding of or receptiveness to the points you are conveying:

- **Asking for clarification:** "Does anyone have any questions?"

- **Seeking affirmation:** "How does that sound?"

- **Confirming understanding:** "Is this clear?"

- **Gauging progress:** "How are we doing so far?"
- **Aligning with priorities:** "Is this something you think your employees would enjoy?"

You can engage your audience by inviting opinions, soliciting feedback, or posing an open-ended question to encourage participation:

- What are your initial reactions to what we've covered so far?
- Does this resonate with the challenges you've experienced?
- How might this approach apply to your team?

Avoid using a section divider if the section only contains one content slide—consider integrating single content slides into a broader section that makes narrative sense. Too many small sections can fragment the story and make it hard for your audience to follow. For shorter decks (fewer than about 10 slides), it may be best to omit section-divider slides altogether.

To Number—Or Not to Number?

You should consider numbering sections in a slide deck when the progression is critical, such as phased plans or when you want to emphasize milestones. Numbers can also make it easier to reference specific sections during a discussion or when the deck is being read. However, numbering sections can add unnecessary complexity and visual clutter, so only use them when they can add clarity.

Example Section-Divider Slides without Numbers

- Market Overview and Trends
- Portfolio Performance Highlights
- Financial Results and Metrics
- Strategic Outlook and Priorities

Example Section-Divider Slides with Numbers

1. Understanding the Current Challenges
2. Designing the New Structure

3. Implementing the Transition Plan

4. Measuring Success and Adjusting

Two Types of Section-Divider Slides

Section-divider slides typically fall into two main types—chapter dividers and repeating agendas—each helping guide your audience through the deck.

- **Chapter-divider slides** introduce new sections or topics. These slides contain the title that reflects the upcoming content and may include a graphic that complements the section content. To reinforce your organization's brand, you can incorporate logos, colors, and visuals tied to your brand identity. If you use a background image, add overlays (e.g., semi-transparent colors to make the text stand out). Keep the overall design minimalist to maintain focus on the section title. The example shows one approach to designing a chapter-divider slide.

This chapter-divider slide includes a solid color on the left to display the section title (Revenue Trends), while the right side features a full-bleed photograph that adds visual interest. Divider slides like this are particularly effective in longer decks where distinct sections need to be clearly separated.

- **Repeating agenda slides** reintroduce the presentation's structure by displaying the full agenda and visually emphasizing the section being covered. This helps reorient the audience, especially in longer or more complex presentations.

  You can highlight the section about to be covered a variety of ways: by bolding or coloring the section title, using an icon or graphic to draw attention to it, shading the current section while dimming the others, or adding a progress indicator like a timeline or numbered steps to show where the audience is in the presentation flow. The example shows one way to visually highlight the current section.

In the example, the darker opportunity box signals the current section, while the other text is grayed out to show what has already been covered and what still lies ahead. By revisiting this slide at transition points in the deck, the presenter helps the audience stay oriented and see how each section connects to the overall flow. Although a repeating agenda slide resembles an agenda slide, you can omit the word *Agenda* on the slide (i.e., you don't need a heading on the slide).

Do You Always Need Section-Divider Slides?

No. You don't always need section dividers, but you should make the structure of your deck clear to your audience. You may consider omitting section divider slides in the following situations:

- The deck is short.
- The sections flow naturally, and dividers could interrupt the flow.
- The deck is intended for reference, and headline connections are more helpful than dividers.
- You use brief summary slides to close each section and transition to the next.
- You include trackers that show progress through the deck's structure.

Closing Slide

Consider including a closing slide that reinforces your communication objective. A closing is your final opportunity to influence what the audience knows, believes, decides, does, or feels. Common tactics generally include some combination of general courtesies, next steps, a brief recap, and/or added perspective.

The following examples could be adapted for slide text or spoken delivery, depending on the context and the deck's density.

General Courtesies: Acknowledge your audience and express gratitude so that you can leave your audience with a feeling of appreciation and goodwill.

- **Feel**: "We appreciate your trust and engagement as we face this together."
- **Believe**: "Your involvement reinforces our shared commitment to addressing this issue effectively."

Next Steps: Outline clear follow-up actions or decisions that need to be made. This approach helps the audience know what's expected and how to proceed.

- **Act**: "Your immediate action: Coordinate with department heads to execute the communication plan starting tomorrow."
- **Decide**: "We need a decision today on allocating resources to the response team, so we can move forward without delay."

The slide below summarizes recommended next steps and invites discussion or approval.

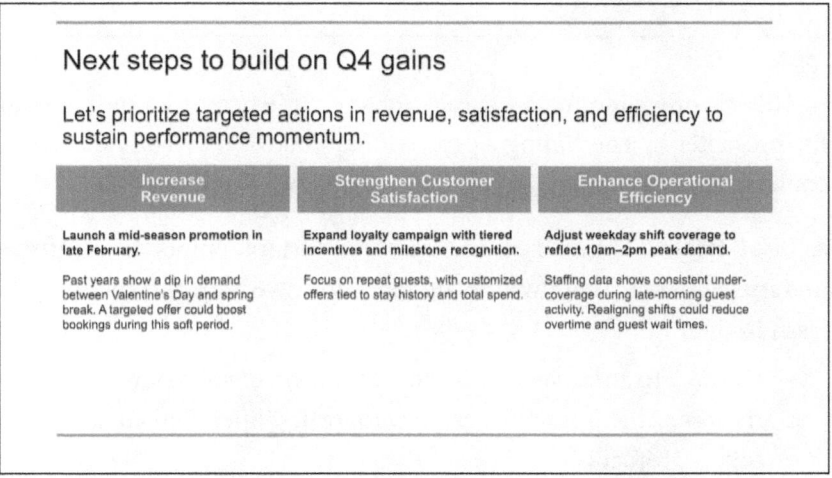

This slide presents steps across three strategic areas. In some cases, the presenter may ask the audience to approve the direction; in others, the goal may be to prompt direct action. As author Daniel Pink suggests, "Clarity on how to think without clarity on how to act can leave people unmoved."[1]

Another option is to include a final closing slide with your contact information. This gives your audience an easy way to follow up and reinforces your openness to continued conversation.

Please contact me with any questions

Andrew B. Quagliata, PhD
Senior Lecturer
Cornell University
SC Johnson College of Business
335 Statler Hall
Ithaca, NY 14853
www.andrewquagliata.com

This closing slide makes it easy for the audience to follow up with the presenter by combining a professional photo with clearly displayed contact information.

A Brief Recap: Summarize the most important points to reinforce understanding. This allows the audience to leave with the key insights fresh in their mind.

- **Know**: "To summarize: The key takeaways include our updated risk assessment framework, new reporting lines, and communication protocols."

- **Believe**: "The case studies we reviewed today demonstrated how similar organizations successfully managed comparable crises with this approach."

A detailed closing summary isn't usually necessary when the slide deck includes an executive summary up front.

Added Perspective: Leave the audience with a powerful statement, quote, or story that inspires belief in your recommendations or evokes an emotional response.

- **Feel:** "While these events have tested us, they have also revealed our strengths and ability to adapt under pressure."
- **Act:** "The choices we make today will determine how effectively we recover and rebuild in the weeks and months ahead."

Question-and-Answer Placeholder Slide

If you are taking questions at the close of a presentation to a live audience, consider including a placeholder slide for the question-and-answer session. As you answer questions, you might navigate back to slides you have already presented—and forward to slides that you've prepared after the placeholder slide that anticipate questions from the audience.

What do you want your audience to see while you are answering questions? You might want your audience to see your closing slide during the question-and-answer session, and if that is the case, omit a Q&A placeholder. However, if you would like them to see something else, consider one of the following three options.

Option 1—Invite Questions: To signal that the presentation has concluded and the floor is open for discussion, you might display a simple prompt such as "Question & Answers," "Q&A," or "What questions do you have?" on the slide. The example below shows one way to visually invite audience questions.

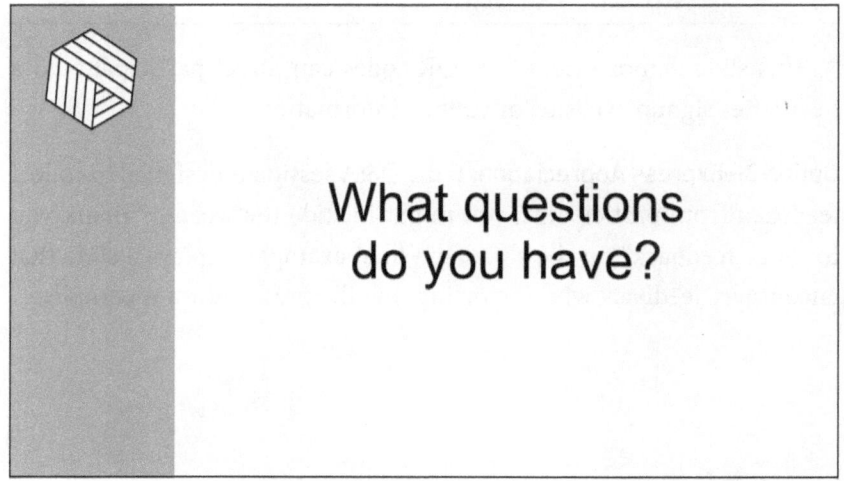

What questions
do you have?

Including a dedicated Q&A slide reduces ambiguity and prevents your last content slide from lingering too long on screen. This placeholder can be especially effective in prompting quieter groups to engage. If you anticipate revisiting earlier content or presenting optional backup material, this slide provides a clear pausing point before navigating elsewhere in the deck.

Option 2—Offer a Way to Follow Up: Some presenters use the Q&A placeholder to encourage continued engagement, such as connecting on LinkedIn or accessing additional resources. The next example shows how a QR code can make it easy for participants to follow up.

This slide demonstrates how QR codes can direct participants to a newsletter signup, website, or contact information.

Option 3—Express Appreciation: If the Q&A session is designed to collect feedback from participants, you might include the words, "Thank you for your feedback" on the slide. The final example displays a slide that encourages feedback while signaling that the presentation is complete.

This variation signals appreciation for feedback from the audience.

Regardless of which approach you choose, keep the design minimalistic.

Question-and-Answer Slides

Although you may feel some apprehension as you prepare for audience questions, thoughtful preparation can help you approach the Q&A session with confidence. While much of your focus during Q&A will be on listening and responding in the moment, a few well-prepared slides can make your answers more effective.

Here are a few strategies to help you prepare slides specifically for your Q&A session:

- **Anticipate common questions.** Start by thinking through the types of questions your audience is likely to ask. These often fall into predictable categories such as requests for additional information or clarifications.

You might expect a question like, "Can you give us a breakdown of the costs?" In that case, consider preparing a slide with a detailed cost breakdown chart that goes beyond what you shared in your main presentation. For clarification questions, such as "What do you mean by customer sentiment?" you could create a slide with an alternative explanation or a graphic to simplify the concept.

Collect more material than you'll likely use. The time you spend preparing responses will increase your confidence—even if the audience never asks those exact questions.

- **Prepare for disagreement or resistance.** If you anticipate skepticism about your recommendations or your idea's feasibility, prepare slides that address common objections. You might create one slide that addresses logical counterarguments, another to address practical considerations like timing or resources, and a third to acknowledge potential cultural differences. Having these slides ready helps you respond calmly without becoming defensive.

Perhaps even more importantly, the time you spend anticipating the questions and developing thoughtful responses is time well spent, even if the audience doesn't ask you the specific questions you prepare for. This preparation helps you feel more confident and ready to handle whatever comes your way.

Create your Q&A slides with the same professionalism and attention to detail as the rest of your deck. Strive to match the overall information density and design style of your presentation. If you want your slides to reflect well on you, they should not be haphazardly thrown together.

Pro Tip: If you are preparing a deck for a live presentation and realize—during rehearsal or revision—that some slides don't fit due to time constraints, consider moving those slides to your Q&A section rather than deleting them. If you've already done the work to create a slide, keep it in your back pocket—you might find it useful later.

Second Closing Slide

In presentations that include a question-and-answer session, don't let your response to the last question be the last thing your audience hears. Consider including a second closing slide that reinforces your main message before you give up the floor. This might mean displaying your original closing slide or creating an entirely new second closing slide. During many of my workshops, I'll take questions at the end, but I will include a second closing slide after the Q&A to provide advice about how to take what participants have learned and apply it or to inspire participants to think differently about their communication.

Frequently Asked Questions (FAQ) Slides

If your audience will read your deck, an approach you could take (while not that common) is to include a frequently-asked-questions section. You could include one slide that provides a summary list of the questions and provides answers on subsequent slides. Another approach would be to list individual questions in the heading section of the slide and use the body area of the slide to answer the question. To create these slides, follow the same design principles discussed in Part II of this book.

Appendices

Include appendices if you have information that is too detailed to include in the body of the slide deck. Common appendices include large data displays, tables of raw data, detailed drawings, definitions, and endnotes.

How to Decide: You might choose to place some information as appendices, rather than in the body of your deck, for a variety of reasons:

- The information may be so detailed and perhaps lengthy that it might be intrusive or interruptive if you were to place it in the middle. (That is, if you were to place the information in the body of your deck, it might distract your audience from the essential argument that you are unfolding.)

- The information may be secondary in importance—nonessential for the body of the argument that you are unfolding within the middle.

- The information addresses questions that might or might not arise in the readers' minds.

How to Present: Present appendices by placing atop each slide the appendix letter followed by title. Here are some examples:

- Appendix A: Definitions
- Appendix B: Reconciliation of Non-GAAP Measures

Each appendix should begin on a new slide.

Bookend Slide

For the final slide of the deck, consider including a bookend slide that doesn't resemble a content slide. Just as a title slide signals the beginning of a slide deck, a final placeholder slide helps signal the end of the deck.

When presenting, consider using a bookend slide to avoid accidentally revealing other content. If you advance past the closing slide, a bookend slide keeps you in presentation mode, preventing unpolished content—such as speaker notes and hidden slides—from appearing on screen.

The bookend slide should support the slide deck's overall visual style. A slide with a colored background that matches your deck's color scheme often works well. One or more of the following approaches may be appropriate:

- **Reinforce the brand:** Add a logo, tagline, and photographs.
- **Contact information:** Include details such as the company address, website, and phone number.
- **Legal disclaimers:** Use copyright or confidentiality language as needed.
- **About the company:** Provide a brief description of the company.

Tanger Factory Outlets Bookend Slide

Tanger Factory Outlet Centers, Inc. (NYSE: SKT) is a leading operator of upscale open-air outlet centers that owns (or has an ownership interest in) and/or manages a portfolio of 37 centers with an additional center currently under development. Tanger's operating properties are located in 20 states and in Canada, totaling approximately 14.0 million square feet, leased to over 2,700 stores operated by more than 600 different brand name companies. The Company has more than 41 years of experience in the outlet industry and is a publicly traded REIT. For more information on Tanger Outlet Centers, call 1-800-4TANGER or visit the Company's website at www.TangerOutlets.com.

Chapter 8 Takeaways

- Special-purpose slides—like title slides, executive summaries, agendas, and section dividers—help readers navigate and absorb the message.

- An executive summary enables selective reading and decision-making; it should be self-sufficient and high in skim value.

- Agenda and table of contents slides preview the structure of a deck; choose points over topics when clarity is a priority.

- Section-divider slides signal transitions and reinforce structure in longer or more complex decks.

- A strong closing slide can recap key points, signal next steps, or inspire action and belief.

- Prepared Q&A slides help you navigate the unexpected with confidence.

- Appendices provide optional depth—without cluttering your main message.

At this point, you've built a complete slide deck—both the content slides that tell your story and the special-purpose slides that support it. Now it's time to take a closer look at each individual slide and fine-tune the details.

Fine-Tune Within Each Slide

Stella thought she was done. She had just emailed the final version of the performance review deck to her manager—thirty slides analyzing revenue, labor costs, and renovation impact across the hotel portfolio. Headlines in place. Data accurate. Charts clean. She even used the company's updated template. Solid work.

Ten minutes later, her manager replied, "This is close, but it still needs polish."

Polish? Stella blinked at the screen. Wasn't that what she'd been doing for the past three hours?

Then came the follow-up call. Her manager walked through three slides as examples:

- "See how this text block fills the whole width? Try breaking it into a bulleted list—it'll be easier to scan."

- "This chart's fine, but it needs an annotation to highlight the key trend."

- "And check the alignment on this page. Right now, everything's just slightly … off."

Stella hadn't missed the numbers. She'd missed the finish.

This chapter is about the finish.

As you review each slide, ask how it helps you achieve your purpose for communicating. If you can't immediately answer the question, you may consider modifying or removing the slide.

Removing is easy; press delete. However, rather than instinctively deleting a slide, you should consider moving it to the end of the deck and hiding it, just in case you change your mind later.

In this chapter, we'll start by checking on promises. Because every slide heading makes a promise, we need to check to make sure those promises are kept. Then, we'll focus on fine-tuning the body of each slide. Small adjustments can significantly improve how your audience processes the information.

Check on Promises

Every content slide makes a promise. It explicitly or implicitly conveys a point that the rest of the slide supports. But does your content deliver on that promise? Or does your audience read the heading, look at what follows, and question whether the support truly backs it up?

As you polish your deck, check each promise your slides make, and ensure they fulfill that promise. If your heading claims, "Market expansion is driving revenue growth," but only the new locations are listed, the slide body isn't keeping the promise. To keep the promise, you might add sales performance data from the new market so that you show their contribution to total revenue. If your heading reads, "Revenue Growth Strategy," but only includes a breakdown of last year's revenue sources with no forward-looking strategy, you might change the heading to "Revenue Performance Review."

Here's how to check your slide promises:

1. **Read the heading and nothing else.** Ask yourself if the heading sets the expectation for what the slide should prove or explain. If so, what is that expectation?

2. **Scan the slide body content.** Does it deliver on what the heading promises? If the two elements do not align, revise either one.

   a. Revise the heading when the supporting content is appropriate, but the heading needs to make a broader or more precise point.

   b. Revise the content when the heading conveys your point precisely, but you need to change or add supporting details.

If the slide body does not deliver on the implicit promise that the heading conveys, you'll sometimes have to revise the heading and the content. For example, you may realize you want to make a more precise point (read = change the heading) and this may require you to cut some of the supporting details.

Why Do Promises Go Unkept?

If the slide body does not keep the promise that the heading conveys, it's usually for one of three reasons:

1. **The heading was written before the content was finalized.** A heading was drafted in the planning stage, but as the deck evolved, the planned content no longer supports the original point or is missing.

2. **The content isn't specific enough.** A slide makes a point like "Customer Reviews Are Improving" but only includes anecdotal evidence rather than numerical data.

3. **The slide tries to do too much.** A slide makes a point, but if the slide is cluttered with multiple, loosely connected supporting details, the promise can become diluted.

Once you check to see that all your headings are appropriately supported, you are ready to fine-tune the body of the slide.

Fine-Tune the Slide Body

The *data-ink ratio* is a useful way to approach fine-tuning the body of your slides. Introduced by Edward Tufte in the context of data visualization, this principle suggests that every graphic element should communicate meaningful content—everything else is unnecessary clutter.[1] While Tufte focused on charts and graphs, the same idea applies to slide design: Every element on the slide should earn its place.

Your goal is to maximize the amount of meaningful information (i.e., data) the slide conveys while minimizing unnecessary or decorative elements (i.e., ink). A high data-ink ratio means more of the slide is devoted to meaningful information. In contrast, a low data-ink ratio means the slide includes too much visual noise—unnecessary borders, shading embellishments, or excessive text that distracts from the message.

The goal is to make every part of your slide purposeful. Sometimes that means removing distractions; other times, it means adding the detail or context your audience needs to fully grasp your message.

As you fine-tune a content slide, you should make intentional choices about its layout, text, and graphic elements.

To consider all these details at once can be too much to juggle simultaneously. A helpful way to approach fine-tuning your deck is to begin by thinking broadly about the layout of each slide. Next, get into specifics surrounding text, and, finally, polish the graphic elements.

Fine-Tune the Layout

Take one last look at how many ideas you're asking your audience to absorb. We first explored this in chapter 4 and came back to it in chapter 7, but it's worth a final check. Is your slide carrying two or three clean chunks of information—or are five or six fighting for attention? You can't out-design a slide that's overloaded. If it feels cluttered, the problem might not be your layout. It might be that you've crammed in too much.

Once you've confirmed your slide isn't carrying more than it can handle, it's time to make sure your audience can follow it. Consider how your audience's eyes will move across the screen or page. Eye-tracking studies show that viewers tend to process information in predictable patterns—left to right and top to bottom, often starting in the upper-left corner.

As you fine-tune your slide's layout, ask yourself three questions to assess the visual hierarchy:

1. Where do I want the audience to look first, and does the slide guide their attention there?

2. Does the most important element stand out clearly from the rest of the content?

3. Does the layout lead the audience naturally through the information in a logical order?

When slides contain multiple chunks of information, don't leave reading order to chance. Simple cues like numbers or lines can help guide the audience's attention. For instance, a vertical line between columns signals a top-down reading order, while a horizontal line between rows suggests a left-to-right reading sequence.

The graphic below depicts two example layouts. The example on the left uses numbers to signal a top-down reading order. The example on the right uses a horizontal line to encourage a left-to-right flow. Without cues like these, audiences may not follow the intended sequence.

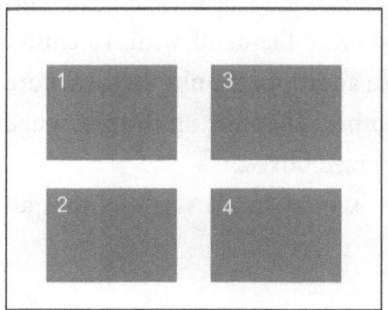 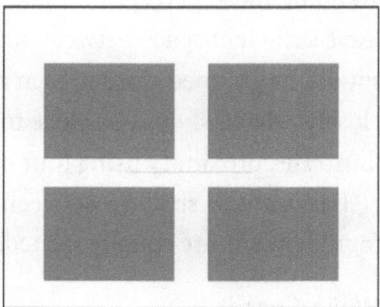

Only use visual cues when you think your audience might be uncertain about how to read the slide. When used thoughtfully, numbers and lines can direct attention without adding noise. But when they're unnecessary, they become clutter

Minimizing distractions is part of the goal, but achieving clarity requires making choices that guide the audience's attention and enhance their understanding. Design principles like alignment, proximity, white space, contrast, and balance are tools that can help in this process. You met some of these principles back in chapter 7 when we looked at slide layouts. Now it's time to use them to fine-tune each slide.[2]

Alignment

By aligning every element on a slide—text, graphics, and design elements—you ensure that everything lines up neatly with something else. Proper alignment creates a sense of order that makes it easier for your audience to process information on a slide. Misaligned elements can distract your audience from your message.

Start by making sure that each information chunk lines up with at least one other element on the slide. Chunks can align with slide headings or subheadings, or they can align with one another.

Proximity

Your audience will perceive elements that are close together as related. To guide those perceptions, place related elements near each other and leave sufficient space between unrelated ones. Elements within a chunk should be grouped close to each other. In addition, chunks that are more closely related should be close to each other. The slide on the next page illustrates proximity using four equally sized boxes.

Because the spacing between boxes is uniform, it suggests that all four elements are equally related.

White Space

Unused space on a slide—white space or negative space—provides audiences with visual relief. You can help prevent a slide from feeling overcrowded by increasing the space between information chunks and leaving margins around the edges of the slide.

Because white space improves readability, you should avoid filling every inch of the slide. By adding white space, you help the most important information stand out.

Q4 initiatives delivered higher guest value at lower operating cost

Upsell Conversion Campaign

- **Action**: Trained front-line staff to identify upgrade opportunities and offer tailored upsells.
- **Result**: Contributed to a 12% increase in average transaction value compared to Q3.

Amenity Restocking Optimization

- **Action**: Moved from automatic to on-request restocking of nonessentials.
- **Result**: Cut supply waste by 27% and reduced replenishment costs.

Localized Social Promotions

- **Action**: Rolled out geo-targeted social media campaigns tied to seasonal events.
- **Result**: Drove a 19% lift in local guest walk-ins during December weekends.

Employee Recognition Pilot

- **Action**: Launched a weekly peer-nominated recognition program tied to guest feedback.
- **Result**: Correlated with a 6-point rise in customer satisfaction among recognized teams.

Contrast

Contrast refers to the visual distinction between elements that helps your audience notice and differentiate them. You can create contrast through color, size, weight, shape, or other attributes.

Resist the urge to use color to contrast chunks within a layout. Instead, reserve color for emphasis—such as calling attention to key words, important phrases, or section headers (i.e., not sentences and paragraphs). This strategy helps you use color as a tool for emphasis without compromising readability.

Build in high contrast between the slide background and all slide elements. High-contrast text requires less effort to read, compared to overly saturated backgrounds that can cause visual strain over time.

- **Choose colors with adequate contrast.** If you opt to use colored backgrounds, maintain sufficient contrast between the background and text color. For example, black text on a white background is easiest to read, while yellow text on a pale background can be difficult to distinguish. Tools like the Web Content Accessibility Guidelines (WCAG) can help you evaluate whether your color combinations meet recommended contrast ratios for readability.[3]

- **Test readability.** Not all readers perceive colors in the same way, so gather feedback from peers to help identify content that may be difficult to read due to color choices.

- **Consider accessibility.** Use accessible color schemes to make your content more inclusive to people with low vision or color blindness. These individuals may find it challenging to read text on colored backgrounds, especially if the contrast is low or the color combinations are difficult to differentiate.

Balance

Balance is a design principle that's often misunderstood. While you don't typically want a content slide that is completely out of balance (all the content on one side with half the slide empty), you also don't need perfect symmetry. Let your content drive your layout, not the other way around. Don't split up related information just to make both sides look equal. Forced balance can make your message difficult to follow. The following example shows how a slide can feel balanced even when the elements aren't symmetrical.

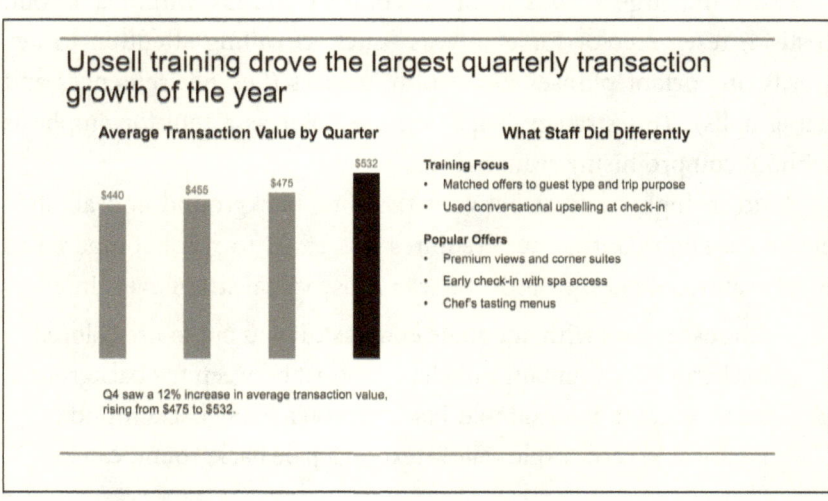

The previous slide includes two chunks: one on the left and one on the right. They are top aligned, but the left chunk extends to the footer, where the right one stops midway down. This layout feels balanced because the alignment and spacing are intentional, even though the elements differ in size.

Fine-Tune the Layout

Use this checklist to evaluate the layout of each slide:
- Does the slide guide the audience's attention to the right starting point?
- Does the important content stand out clearly?
- Are related elements grouped closely together?
- Are unrelated elements spaced apart to signal different chunks?
- Is every element aligned with something else on the slide?
- Is there enough breathing room around the content?
- Is the content visually balanced, or does one side feel heavier than the other?
- Does this layout support the message clearly—or was it chosen out of habit?

Fine-Tune the Text

The most common mistake people make with slide text is including too much of it. Let's begin by reviewing how you can phrase the text concisely and then how to present it appropriately.

Text Phrasing

By phrasing ideas clearly and concisely, you enable your audience to understand your meaning quickly, easily, and unambiguously. As you edit your phrasing, use the table on the next page to help you spot common issues.

Common Text Phrasing Issues

Focus Area	What to Look For	Quick Fixes & Why They Matter
Words	Vague or abstract nouns	Replace abstractions with concrete terms: "operational efficiencies" → "cuts check-in time by 90 seconds."
	Weak verbs (*is/are, has*)	Swap weak verbs for actions: "Revenue increased 8%," not "Revenue experienced an 8% increase." Clear, specific words improve comprehension and recall.
Phrases	Redundant pairs ("completely unanimous")	Delete overlap: "unanimous."
	Wordy opener ("In order to ...")	Streamline: "To reduce," not "In order to." Readers under time pressure process concise text faster.
Sentences	Lines that run past ~20 words	Break or combine for an 8- to 15-word target; mix lengths for rhythm.
	Passive constructions that hide the doer	Use active voice when you can: "Guests broke 12 plates" clarifies agency and trims words.
Lists	Bullets that start with different parts of speech	Begin each item with the same verb form ("Increase," "Introduce," "Enhance").
	Numbered lists that don't imply order	Use numbers only for steps or rank order. Parallel structure boosts skim value.
Tone	Overstatements ("always," "never")	Hedge where appropriate: "may improve" vs. "will revolutionize."
	Unnecessary jargon or acronyms	Spell out or define acronyms on first use unless they're obvious to the audience.

Work through one focus area at a time—first spotting common trouble signs, then applying the quick fixes. By the end, you'll have stripped out the clutter, tightened the prose, and left only the language that earns its keep.

When you think the wording is set, do one more thing: Read the slide out loud. If the phrasing flows, you'll glide through it without extra breaths. If you stumble, the slide is telling you it still needs work. By reading aloud, you experience the text the same way your audience will. Keep tightening until you can read every line comfortably in a single pass.

Text Presentation

To fine-tune how you present text on a slide, use the following design principles: space, alignment, contrast, and repetition.

Space

Text needs space. Without it, even the best ideas will be difficult for audiences to process. In traditional documents, spacing usually refers to the space between lines of text. On slides, spacing includes that—but also the white space around text blocks, between headings and paragraphs, and between chunks of information. Effective spacing improves readability and helps your audience process information more quickly.

One of the most common space-related mistakes is including too much text in a single paragraph. Whether you're working with a low-, medium-, or high-density slide deck, audiences may not expect paragraphs, but they do expect clarity. In fact, you should avoid using paragraphs altogether in low- and medium-density decks. In high-density decks, use them sparingly, and break longer paragraphs into shorter, more digestible blocks.

Instead of using dense blocks of text, aim for key words, phrases, brief sentences, and bulleted lists. Bulleted lists work particularly well because they naturally create white space—each item typically ends before reaching the right margin, leaving visual breathing room that makes it easier to scan. However, be sure you are using them appropriately:

- Use bulleted lists only when you have two or more items.
- Introduce each bulleted list with a grammatically complete statement.
- Keep all bulleted list items parallel in phrasing.

- Keep the left margin consistent for all items that extend beyond a single line.
- Avoid using single-item bullets.
  ‣ Avoid using second-level bullets (like this one).
- Use a numbered list when sequence is important.
- Consider adding extra spacing between bullet points to keep them from crowding together.

Reduce Eye Sweeps and Return Sweeps

Both horizontal and vertical eye movements add to cognitive load and reduce comprehension. By paying attention to line length and paragraph structure, you can help your audience absorb information more easily.

When a line of text stretches too far across a slide, your audience is forced to make long eye sweeps—the horizonal movement from the start to the end of a line. When a paragraph contains too many lines, your audience must also make frequent return sweeps—the vertical jump back to the left margin to start a new line.

When polishing your text, look for opportunities to reduce both types of sweeps:

- Shorter lines reduce the horizontal effort but can increase return sweeps.
- Fewer lines reduce vertical efforts but may require longer horizontal sweeps.

Aim for a balance between line length and paragraph depth by keeping your text boxes within one-third and two-thirds the width of the slide and adjusting the number of lines accordingly. The following table offers a general guide for how many lines to include based on the width of the text box.

Text Box Width Guidelines

Text Box Width	Max Number of Lines
1/3 width	4 lines
1/2 width	5 lines
2/3 width	6 lines

Use as many lines as necessary to make your point clear—but as few as possible to avoid visually overloading your audience.[4]

Skip Borders Around Text—Use Space Instead

When you need to separate or organize text on a slide, avoid defaulting to borders or boxes around blocks of text. While these elements might seem like a useful way to display information, they often add visual clutter. Borders can interrupt the natural flow, making it harder for your audience to absorb the content.

Here's why borders often do more harm than good:

- According to cognitive load theory, unnecessary visual elements can increase mental effort, making it harder for the audience to process and retain information.

- The Gestalt principle of simplicity tells us that readers tend to organize visual elements into simple, orderly groups. Borders interrupt that natural tendency by fragmenting the slide into too many separate units.

- Usability studies underscore the importance of visual hierarchy and flow in guiding the reader's eyes through the content in a logical sequence. When readers' eyes encounter a border, they do not move smoothly from one chunk to the next.

Instead of using borders, use white space and subtle visual cues to separate text.

Spacing creates natural boundaries that are easier for the eye to navigate. You can also use cues like typeface choices, size, color, text placement, and lines to establish a clear visual hierarchy that guides your audience's eye through the content, rather than relying on borders to make distinctions. For example, in the slide below, observe how the natural reading flow is disrupted with borders around nine different blocks of text.

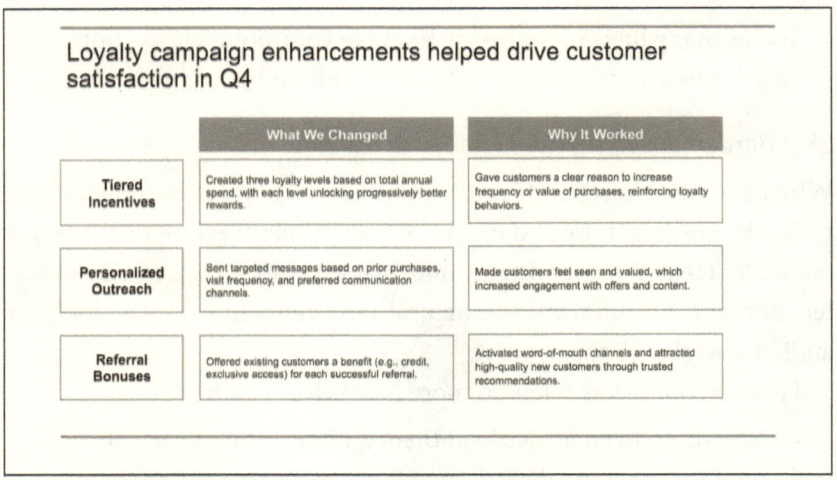

In this example, borders create unnecessary visual clutter and suggest each block should be read independently. In contrast, the borders on the next slide have have been removed and replaced with horizontal lines between rows, encouraging a smoother, more intuitive reading path—left to right, then top down.

The slide on the next page shows how layout and spacing alone can communicate structure more effectively than borders. With two low-contrast divider lines instead of enclosing boxes, the slide feels lighter, and the audience can process relationships between content blocks more easily. The white space guides the eye without interference.

Loyalty campaign enhancements helped drive customer satisfaction in Q4

	What We Changed	Why It Worked
Tiered Incentives	Created three loyalty levels based on total annual spend, with each level unlocking progressively better rewards.	Gave customers a clear reason to increase frequency or value of purchases, reinforcing loyalty behaviors.
Personalized Outreach	Sent targeted messages based on prior purchases, visit frequency, and preferred communication channels.	Made customers feel seen and valued, which increased engagement with offers and content.
Referral Bonuses	Offered existing customers a benefit (e.g., credit, exclusive access) for each successful referral.	Activated word-of-mouth channels and attracted high-quality new customers through trusted recommendations.

Polish Your Paragraph Spacing

As you fine-tune the spacing of your text, consider three more choices that can impact the readability of your slides.

- **Keep your spacing consistent.** Don't let one block of text breathe while another gasps for air.

- **Skip the indent on multi-line text**. Slide body text works best with clean, left-aligned text.

- **Use one space after a period.** Two spaces made sense when we used typewriters with fixed-width typefaces. Today's software adds the right amount of space automatically; two spaces can make your slides feel like they time-traveled from the typewriter era.

When text is spaced consistently and appropriately, your audience can absorb more information with less effort.

Alignment

For most slide text, left alignment is the clearest and most reader-friendly choice. A clear left edge and uneven right margin make it easier for the audience to read.[4] Use the following guidelines to apply alignment effectively:

- Left-align slide headings and subheading text. Avoid centering them.

- Left-align slide body text. Don't justify the text (i.e., align both edges), as it can create uneven spacing between words and reduce readability.

- Left-align segment headings and the text beneath them. If you choose to center segment headings, apply that choice consistently across the slide.

Align blocks of text with other slide elements. Line up blocks of text with nearby elements such as charts and images. Don't allow text to drift into the slide margin. Avoid overlapping text with other elements.

Contrast

By building in contrast, you can help your audience to distinguish one piece of text from another by making the most important content stand out. Choices in font size, weight, and color can create a visual hierarchy that supports your message and makes it easier for your audience to process what they see.

Use Contrast to Emphasize Key Elements

- **Size:** Use larger font sizes for headings or key numbers. For example, if your slide contains a key metric like "Sales increased 24%," consider displaying the number in a larger size than the surrounding text.

- **Weight:** Use bold text to emphasize important words or phrases, such as recommendations or calls to action. But use bold sparingly—if everything is bold, nothing stands out.

- **Color:** Introduce color variations to highlight key text, especially on data-heavy slides. For instance, in a table with several numbers, making one number a different color will immediately draw attention. In addition, use dark text to emphasize important content and light text to make less critical information fade.

Direct Attention Without Overdoing It

Too much contrast—especially when introduced inconsistently—can make a slide feel chaotic. A slide with multiple colors, font sizes, and bolding styles can distract or confuse your audience. To apply contrast effectively

- Choose one or two elements to emphasize per slide.
- Use contrast consistently across your deck (e.g., bold is always used for segment headings, color is always used for data highlights).
- Avoid using contrast purely for decoration. Every contrast choice should serve a clear purpose.

When using color to create contrast, pair color with another cue, like bold or a size difference, to support accessibility for people with low vision or color blindness.

I'm often asked if it's a good idea to bold individual words or phrases within a sentence or emphasize key ideas. At first glance, this seems like a smart way to guide attention. But in practice, it's often more distracting than helpful.

In many decks, bolding appears arbitrary—the logic behind the choices isn't clear. Instead of reinforcing the message, bolding can become visual noise. In some cases, it can feel like a substitute for effective writing—like a visual crutch used to rescue an otherwise unclear sentence.

Instead of bolding excessively, use it sparingly, especially within sentences. If you decide to bold key words, keep the following suggestions in mind:

1. **Consider other techniques first.** Before bolding, ask yourself whether a shorter sentence, a new line, or a clearer heading would eliminate the need to bold at all. In many cases, editing the sentence for clarity makes bolding unnecessary.

2. **Have a clear reason for each bolded phrase.** Ask yourself whether someone who only saw the bolded text would still understand the key takeaway of the sentence or slide. If they wouldn't understand, you may be bolding the wrong things or too many things.

3. **Limit to one bolded segment per sentence.** More than one bolded phrase per sentence can pull the audience's attention in too many directions.

4. **Avoid bolding obvious words.** Don't bold words that are already naturally emphasized by their position or context. For example, bolding "increased" in "Sales increased by 24%" doesn't add value—especially if the number is what you really want your audience to notice.

5. **Test it for skimmability.** Skim the slide and read only the bolded text. If the message is clearer as a result, the bolding is probably working. If it creates confusion or doesn't add clarity, remove it.

Repetition

Repetition in text means applying the same visual logic to similar types of content. On a single slide, consistent formatting makes it easier for your audience to scan and understand your message. Headings look like headings, body text looks like body text, and key elements stand out in predictable ways.

Let's cover four ways to use repetition to make your slide text easier to scan.

Be Consistent With Fonts

Font choice is one of the most visible areas for repetition. Within a slide, use the same font family and apply it consistently to similar elements. For example

- Use the same font type throughout unless a deliberate design choice justifies the variation.
- Make sure each type of text looks the same every time it appears. Body text should match body text, headings should match headings, subheadings should match subheadings, and bullet points should match bullet points.

Even small inconsistencies can subtly undermine the professionalism of a slide.

Use Consistent Capitalization

Choose a capitalization style that supports readability, and apply it consistently within the slide. For headings and subheadings, consider using sentence case, which capitalizes only the first letter of the word and proper nouns. Sentence case is easier to read than title case, which capitalizes the first letter of every major word.[6]

Watch for Short Lines

When possible, avoid ending a paragraph with a single short word on its own line. To create a more cohesive shape on the slide, consider adjusting the line break or slightly rewording the sentence so the final line includes at least two words.

Use Formatting Effects Consistently

Formatting effects like bold, italics, and color secure visual emphasis, but only when used purposefully and repeatedly in the same way. If the same type of content is emphasized in different ways on the same slide, you may inadvertently confuse your audience.

- **Bold:** Use bold primarily for emphasis—especially for segment headings, key phrases, or important data points. Don't bold entire sentences or paragraphs.
- **Italics:** Reserve italics for secondary emphasis, such as a title or specialized term.

- **Color:** Use color to categorize content, such as stages in a process. Assign each piece of content a consistent color and apply it the same way every time it appears.
- **Underline:** Avoid underlining unless you're indicating a hyperlink.
- **ALL CAPS:** Save all-caps formatting for short labels only, such as chart axis titles or segment headings. Avoid using all caps in sentences, which are more difficult to read and can appear overly aggressive.

Fine-Tune the Text Checklist

Use this checklist to review how you phrase and display any text that you place in the body of each slide.

- Is the text phrased clearly, concisely, and in a tone appropriate for the audience?
- Have you used keywords, phrases, or lists instead of full paragraphs when possible?
- Is the amount of text manageable as measured by both line length and number of lines?
- Is all the slide text left-aligned (except when centering is purposeful and consistent)?
- Are key elements emphasized with size, weight, or color (and not cluttered with all three)?
- Is formatting (bold, italics, font size, capitalization) used consistently within the slide?
- If you have used bold within a sentence, is it purposeful and limited?

Now that we've covered how to polish the text, let's turn to fine-tuning the graphic elements on each slide.

Fine-Tune the Graphic Elements

Just like layout and text, graphic elements should be intentional and polished—not presented for the sake of visual appeal or in order to fill space.

Let's begin by reviewing the ways I've seen people use graphics inappropriately. Then we'll look at how to refine your graphics to improve clarity and impact. Finally, we'll explore how to guide your audience's attention with purposeful graphic titles, captions, and annotations.

Avoid Common Missteps

For each graphic that you have added to a slide, step back and ask a critical question: Does this graphic truly help the audience understand your point, or is it just filling space? Far too often, graphic elements compete with the message rather than support it. Here are some common missteps to watch for:

Generic Images: Stock photos of people shaking hands. Light bulbs to signify ideas. Lighthouses to represent clarity.

- **Problem:** These images may seem appropriate at first glance, but they rarely make the message clearer. Instead, they increase the cognitive load by forcing the audience to guess how the image connects to the content.

- **Fix:** Use images only when they directly reinforce the content, such as showing a location, a product, or relevant example.

Overuse or Misuse of Icons: Icons can help visually separate points, but it can be easy to overuse them.

- **Problem:** A bulleted list with an icon next to every line may look polished, but it often distracts from the content rather than clarifying it.

- **Fix:** Use icons sparingly and consistently. Make sure each icon adds meaning. An icon should rarely be larger than the capital letters in the text it accompanies.

Charts Without Insight: Some slides include charts simply because a number exists.

- **Problem:** A chart that shows just one number or a painfully obvious point doesn't add value; it just takes up space.
- **Fix:** Include a chart only when it reveals a pattern, trend, or comparison that's easier for your audience to grasp visually than through text alone.

Maps Without Meaning: Maps can provide helpful context, but only when geography actually matters to your audience.

- **Problem:** Many times, maps on slides function as vague backgrounds—unlabeled dots, unexplained, and disconnected from the point.
- **Fix:** Use maps only when location is essential to the message, and label them clearly so your audience can interpret them at a glance.

Infographics That Prioritize Style over Substance: Some infographics, especially those pulled from AI or websites, look polished but communicate very little.

- **Problem:** Complex, visually dense infographics often prioritize aesthetic design over clear communication. If your audience must work to decode the graphic, it's not doing its job.
- **Fix:** Favor clarity over flair. Simple, well-labeled graphics are more effective than intricate graphics that compete for attention.

Distracting or Dated Visuals: Animated GIFs. Cartoonish clip art. Low-resolution images.

- **Problem:** These visuals damage your credibility. PowerPoint removed clip art in 2010 for a good reason: Audiences associate these visuals with outdated, amateur presentations. If your visual choices feel dated, so will your message.

- **Fix:** Use clean, high-resolution graphics that match the level of professionalism of your message. And if you're tempted to ignore this advice, pause and ask whether the graphic is adding clarity.

Now that you know what to avoid, let's look at how to refine your graphics.

Refine Graphics for Clarity and Impact

Once you have resolved the common missteps, you can focus on stripping away what may distract the audience and strengthen what supports the message.

- **Use contrast to guide attention.** Every graphic should have a clear focal point. Whether that focal point is a key data point in a chart or a critical step in a diagram, your audience should immediately be able to tell what's most important. You can direct your audience's attention by applying contrast through size, shape, color, or position. This is what Dan Roam calls "pre-cognitive attributes."[7] These are visual signals that our brains notice almost instantly.

  Try using visual contrast to

  ▸ Make a single data point stand out in a bar chart (e.g., Use a darker color than the other bars. Our brains think darker colors are more important than lighter colors).

  ▸ Enlarge or bold the text that conveys a critical step in a process diagram.

  ▸ Position the most important visual element in the top left, where eyes often land first.

  One or two contrast cues is usually sufficient.

- **Remove clutter—and simplify.** Most graphics include more details than necessary. Look for opportunities to reduce clutter without removing meaning:

- Remove unnecessary gridlines, backgrounds, and borders that don't add value.

- Eliminate redundant labels, especially when the data point is already clear from context.

- Lighten or delete axes and lines that don't carry essential information.

- Replace legends with direct labeling. Instead of asking your audience to look back and forth between the legend and the data, place labels directly on charts.

  If a graphic, by default, includes shading, gradients, 3-D effects, or drop shadows, remove these visual effects.

- **Maintain graphic consistency.** As you polish, make sure each graphic feels like part of the same presentation, not a collection of borrowed parts. To maintain graphic consistency:

  - Use graphics that follow a common style (e.g., same line weight, font, color palette).

  - Avoid copying graphics from multiple sources. Graphics from different sources (stock images, icons, Google searches) don't usually match in terms of colors, design style, and proportions. These inconsistencies can make your deck seem disjointed.

  - When possible, create or customize graphics yourself so they align with your brand or deck design. Graphics you find from other sources may include information that isn't completely relevant to your deck. By creating your own graphics, you retain full control to adapt visuals for your audience and context.

    If, without permission, you use graphics from a source other than yourself, legal issues involving copyright may arise, especially in client- or public-facing decks.

Check to See You've Used the Most Effective Graphics

Every graphic should earn its space by making the key information immediately obvious and no more complicated than the audience needs. Ask yourself:

- Does this graphic reveal a comparison or just decorate the slide?
- Does the audience really need this much information, or would a simpler format work better?
- Is there a clearer or more intuitive way to visualize this information?

In his book *Say It with Charts*, visual-communication expert Gene Zelazny provides guidance about how to determine the correct chart type when you compare items. Below, I summarize his guidance and expand it to other types of graphics.[8]

When to Use Each Graphic Type

Graphic Type	Best for
Bar	Ranking of items
Line	Changes over time
Column	Items within ranges
Pie	Parts of a whole
Scatter-plot	Relationship between variables
Table (numerical)	Precise values
Process/Sequence Diagram	Steps, stages, or flows
Relationship Diagram	Showing how concepts overlap or compare
Map	Showing geographic data or location-based patterns
Image/Photo	Providing visual example, product, or location

The table below outlines what to check when polishing your graphics, organized by graphic type.

Polishing Graphics

Graphic Type	What to Look for When Polishing
Data Graphics	Remove clutter. Use direct labels. Emphasize key trends.
Process and Sequence Graphics	Make sure steps are clearly numbered or directional.
Relationship Graphics	Make sure lines, arrows, or positioning show how elements relate.
Conceptual/Explanatory	Confirm that your diagram clarifies—not complicates—the idea.
Context and Location	Include meaningful labels.
Image-Based Graphics	Use high-quality images.

Support the Graphic with Text

Even the clearest graphics can sometimes benefit from a bit of explanation. Whether you're introducing a graphic in the body text, giving it a clear title, writing a meaningful caption, or adding on-slide annotations, the right words can reduce the effort required to interpret the graphic. In this section, you'll learn how to decide when each type of text is necessary and how to use it to reinforce your point.

Introduce Graphics

Consider whether the audience needs to be introduced to the graphic to understand its relevance. In some cases, especially with low-density slides, a well-designed graphic may not need written commentary if it's supported by a presenter's verbal explanation. But as the density level of your slides increases, textual references help guide the audience's attention and clarify how the graphic supports the message.

The next three lists can help you decide when, where, and how to reference introductory text.

When to Reference

- The more dense the slide, the more helpful it is to direct the audience explicitly.
- If a slide contains multiple graphics with explanatory text, referencing each can reduce confusion.
- In high-density decks, introducing a graphic in the body text can improve narrative flow.

Where to Reference

- You can reference a graphic either before showing it or after the audience has seen it. In traditional reports, references often come first. In highly visual slide decks, readers may scan the graphic first, especially if it's in a prominent spot (e.g., upper left).
- Either approach is fine. The key is to match the reference with the slide's visual flow.

How to Reference

Use spatial references or graphic titles to orient the audience. For example:

- "As shown in the chart on the left …"
- "The diagram below outlines the process …"
- "The photograph above shows the renovation in progress."
- "In the map titled 'Q2 Regional Expansion' …"

Graphic Titles

The title of a graphic, typically positioned above the graphic, tells the audience what they're looking at. When deciding whether or how to title a graphic, consider the following questions:

- Does the graphic have a title? (Does it need one?)
- Is the title redundant with the slide heading or does it add clarity?

- Is the title a topic title (Q2 Sales) or a message title (Q2 Sales Increased 15% Last Quarter)? Topic titles help audiences understand units of measurement (e.g., currency, time), while message titles reinforce key points.

If the message is already clearly stated in the slide's heading or subheading, a separate graphic title might not be necessary.

Captions

Placed below or beside a graphic, captions offer clarifying details, sources, or contextual notes. Use captions when additional explanations will help your audience interpret the graphic more accurately. Captions can

- Explain subtle aspects of the graphic (e.g., shaded ranges, outliers, projections)
- Provide units of measurement, date ranges, or source citations
- Give the audience a little more help interpreting what they are seeing

If you use captions, make them less visually prominent than body text (i.e., smaller in font size and perhaps even lighter color).

Graphic Annotations

Within or on top of the graphic, you might consider annotations to draw attention to specific elements. These annotations may include comments in text boxes or cues, such as arrows, highlights, or lines. Because annotations act like visual guides that help the audience know where to focus their attention, they are especially helpful for data-heavy graphics like charts or diagrams.

Nancy Duarte suggests five different approaches for annotating data graphics.[7] Each approach offers a different way to clarify your message and direct the audience's attention.

- **Highlight data:** Use contrasting color to draw attention to a specific bar, line, dot, or area in a chart or diagram. This approach works well when you want to emphasize a key data point or compare one item against a baseline or group average.

- **Label data:** Place a text box directly on or near a graphic to make it easier to interpret. Labels make your graphics more skimmable and reduce reliance on legends or axes.
- **Bracket data:** Use brackets, braces, or shaded bands to connect two or more data points and show how they relate.
- **Delineate data:** Draw a line or boundary to separate key areas or illustrate a threshold or benchmark. Delineation is helpful in charts that compare performance against goals.
- **Explode data:** Use the "explode" technique to break out part of the graphic and give it more emphasis or space. When you explode data, you zoom in, pull a segment away from the whole, and isolate part of the graphic for closer examination.

Annotations make your graphics speak. They guide your audience to focus on the most important insight.

Fine-Tune the Graphics Checklist

Use this checklist to evaluate each graphic element on a slide:
- Does this graphic support the message, or is it decorative or distracting?
- Is the correct type of graphic being used to communicate this idea?
- Is the graphic clean and uncluttered (e.g., minimal gridlines, no legends)?
- Have you used contrast (color, size, shape, position) to direct the audience's attention?
- Are all labels and annotations clearly legible and necessary?
- Are graphic styles (icons, lines, fonts, colors) consistent?
- Have you referenced graphics within body text where needed?
- Have you included a helpful title, caption, or annotation where needed?

Try This with AI

Polish an overloaded slide. *Prompt:* "This slide feels too crowded. Can you help me identify what to cut, simplify, or reformat?" [Paste the slide.]

Chapter 9 Takeaways

- Each slide makes a promise—check that your slide body delivers on it.
- Fine-tune the layout to direct attention, highlight key points, and guide the audience through the content.
- Keep text clear, concise, and easy to scan. Use short sentences, lists, and intentional formatting.
- Polish your graphics by removing clutter, emphasizing key insights, and ensuring consistency in style.
- Support your graphics with purposeful text, including titles, captions, and annotations that clarify and reinforce the message.
- Small design choices—like alignment, grouping, and white space—can significantly improve your slide's clarity and professionalism.

When you purposefully use layouts, text, and graphics, they help you produce more effective slides. But even effective slides can lose their impact if they don't work together across the deck. In the final chapter, we will move from polishing individual slides to reviewing your deck as a whole. We'll explore how to fine-tune your deck across slides so that your message builds clearly and cohesively from start to finish.

Strengthen the Story Across the Deck

Susanne worked late all week polishing the final pitch for a major client. As the client project lead at a top consulting firm, she knew how much was riding on this presentation. The opening content slide included a message heading, a simple graphic, and clear supporting points. Slides two and three connected nicely. But by slide eight, things started to unravel.

Font sizes shrank. Margins tightened. A new color appeared. By slide ten, the slide headings changed from messages to topics. It was like watching a movie where the actors kept changing costumes mid-scene, without explanation. The client didn't say anything, but Susanne could feel it. The presentation stopped feeling like a story and started feeling like a slideshow.

This is the kind of dissonance that can derail a presentation. Although each individual slide may be effective, the whole deck doesn't hang together. By fine-tuning across slides, you can create a polished, cohesive deck that sends a signal: This message is well crafted, well considered, and worth your audience's attention.

Once you have refined each individual slide, now it's time for you to zoom out and consider whether the entire deck works as a unified whole. This chapter guides you through three steps:

1. **Assess the structure:** Does the flow of your slides build a clear and coherent message from beginning to end?
2. **Assess the design:** Do your slides look like they belong together, with visual consistency and strong alignment?
3. **Assess the text:** Have you ensured consistency in phrasing, formatting, and tone across the deck?

When each slide contributes to a cohesive experience, your deck becomes more than the sum of its parts. It becomes a story your audience can easily follow and will likely remember.

Assess the Structure

A slide deck isn't a collection of individual slides; it's a sequence designed to accomplish a specific purpose. A well-structured deck has a shape. It builds direction, develops tension, and resolves with clarity, much like a good story.

That kind of shape rarely happens by accident. By the time you reach the polishing stage, you've already made dozens of structural choices, both small and significant. You've decided whether to group individual slides into sections, how to sequence those sections, and how to sequence slides within each section.

Now it's time to step back and ask: Does the whole deck make sense from beginning to end?

One of the best ways to test the structure is surprisingly simple. Read only the slide headings in sequence to check for overall coherence. Don't get distracted by the graphics or supporting text. Do the slide headings form a logical flow of ideas? As you move from one slide to the next, does the narrative hold together, or does it feel more like flipping channels on a TV, jumping from one disconnected topic to the next?

If you struggle to find the connection between content slides, chances are your audience will too. Your slides should unfold like a story; even someone skimming the headings should be able to grasp your main message.

So, before you lock in your deck, assess three organizing principles: grouping, labeling, and sequencing.

Grouping

- Are related ideas grouped together in sections, subsections, or slides next to each other?
- Would your audience expect to see these ideas presented together?
- Are any sections too broad or too narrow?
- Does every section, subsection, and slide serve a clear purpose?

Labeling

- Are your section labels clear?
- Are you labeling sections by topic (Q3 Sales), points (Sales Fell Sharply in Q3), or question (Why Did Q3 Sales Drop?), and sticking to one approach?
- If you're using questions as section titles, are they questions your audience would actually ask?
- Would someone skimming the deck understand what each section is about just from the labels alone?

Sequencing the Story

- Does the order of the sections, subsections, and slides match the audience's needs? Or are you making them work too hard to connect the dots?
- Would someone unfamiliar with the content find this progression intuitive?
- Is the most important information where it needs to be?
- Do your transitions help connect ideas smoothly? Or does it feel like you're jumping from one slide to the next without a bridge?

Because your readers are likely to focus their attention on the slide headings, any extra time that you devote to reviewing your headings is a worthwhile investment.

Try This with AI

Assess the overall flow. *Prompt:* "Here are the headlines from each slide in my deck. Does the flow make sense? What would you change to improve coherence?"

Assess the Design

In a film, we expect each scene to look like part of the same world. That expectation holds even when the setting changes. Your deck works the same way. Design choices like consistent margins, trackers, and typography serve as your deck's visual continuity, helping the audience stay immersed in your message.

Once you've confirmed that the structure of your deck is effective, it's time to make sure the design choices you've made work as a whole. As you review your slides, focus on four areas of design that matter across the deck: density, layout, trackers, and design principles.

Density

Not every slide needs to carry the same amount of content. In fact, it's often helpful if they don't. A high-density deck benefits from the occasional low-density slide to give the audience a breather. And a low-density deck can include the occasional high-density slide, especially if the details are necessary.

The key is intention. Does the overall density of the deck match the expectations of your audience and the demands of the situation?

If you use a high-density slide during a live presentation in which most slides are low density, give your audience extra processing time.

Conversely, if you use a low-density slide in a deck that will be read, and most of the slides are high density, ensure that the low-density slide doesn't need textual elaboration for your audience to understand the point.

Layouts

When preparing slide layouts, people often rely on faulty assumptions. Some individuals think they should never repeat a layout. Others think they must repeat layouts to create consistency.

The best layout for any individual content slide is the one that makes your point most clearly, even if it's the same as the slide before it. Nevertheless, if you find yourself reusing the same layout over and over again, it may be a sign that you haven't fully explored how else the information could be presented on the slide.

For section-divider slide layouts, consistency is key. Use a consistent layout so the audience can easily recognize transitions between sections. You can vary the visuals, such as using a different high-quality photo for each section, but keep the text in the same position on each slide. Style them consistently so the audience can easily recognize transitions.

Trackers

No matter how clear your story is, some people in your audience will still wonder, *Where are we?* Or *How much is left?* Trackers can help answer these questions.

As introduced in chapter 5, trackers are design elements (textual, graphical, or both) that show the audience where they are in your deck. They work like breadcrumb trails or running headers in a report. And while trackers are optional, they're especially helpful in longer presentations, in-person settings where the audience can't flip ahead, and workshops or trainings with multiple sections or learning outcomes.

Consider placing trackers in the bottom-right footer area of a slide. However, if that placement doesn't work for your deck, trackers can be effective in other locations, as long they don't interfere with your message:

- **In the upper-right corner:** A tracker placed here is less likely to compete for attention. One adjustment you may need to make is to reduce the width of your slide heading box so both elements do not overlap.
- **Along the top header:** A tracker placed from margin to margin can be done well if sufficient space is included between the margin and the slide heading and subtle colors are used.
- **Along the bottom footer:** A tracker on the bottom margin is similar to one along the top. It needs sufficient space, so the other content doesn't feel crowded.
- **In the lower-left corner:** A tracker placed here can work when there's no footer text, but the downside is that it often competes with source notes or other footer information.
- **In the upper-left corner:** A tracker placed here can compete for attention with your heading, but it can also be an additional piece of information that your audience finds helpful.

Avoid placing trackers in the left or right margins.

Although you can format trackers in many ways, they all share the same purpose: to subtly show your audience where they are in the structure of the deck. Below are four examples of how I've used trackers in different contexts.

1. **Progress box in the lower right:** In a workshop structured around five learning outcomes, I used a row of small square boxes in the lower-right corner—just to the left of the slide number. The first box was filled at the start, while the others remained empty. As the session progressed to the next section, the next box filled in. The graphic at the top of the next page shows how the progress boxes were placed and how the current section was highlighted.

   This compact approach works well in workshops or trainings, where participants want to track progress but don't need to see section titles.

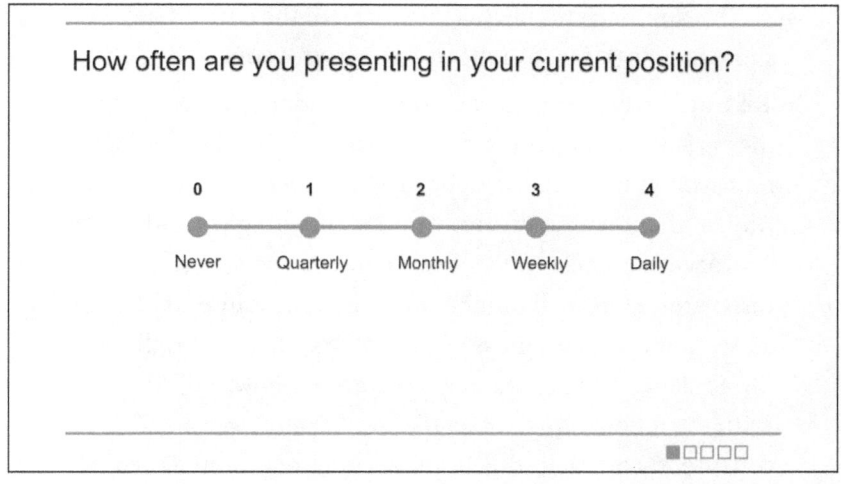

2. **Icons on a connected line:** In a three-section presentation, I used iconography to highlight the current section. I placed a single line with three small circles in the upper-right corner of the slide. Instead of filling in each circle, an icon (larger than the circle) appeared above the current section. The icon represented the theme of the section. As the presentation moved forward, the icon shifted from one circle to the next. The next graphic illustrates how the icon appears above the active section to show progression through the deck.

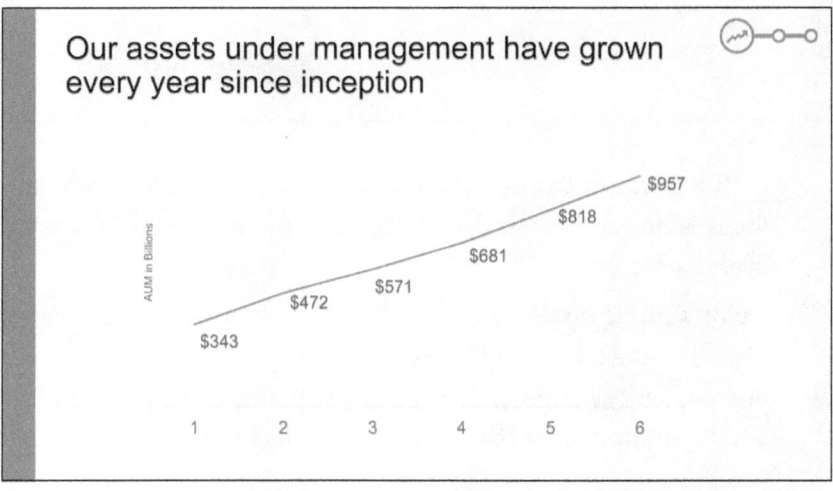

This approach highlights the theme of the current section while showing how it fits into the overall progression of the deck.

3. **Text-only tracker:** Some trackers remind the audience where they are without tracking overall progress. Displaying the current section name in the upper-right corner of a slide is a simple way to orient your audience without crowding the slide. This approach is especially effective when your presentation is structured around a small number of core ideas. Rather than showing all sections like a progress tracker might, this approach reminds the audience which idea they're exploring now.

In the following example, the word "Self-Awareness" appears consistently on each slide in the section, reinforcing the theme without calling too much attention to itself.

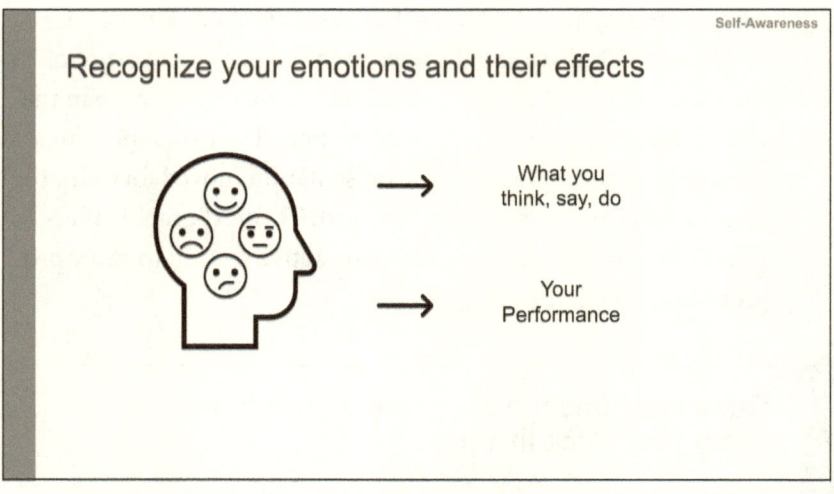

This method works well in concept-driven decks, where the focus is on reinforcing the current idea rather than emphasizing overall progress.

4. **Color-shifting boxes across the top:** In a keynote with three main ideas, I used a thin row of boxes at the top of the slide. Only one box was dark at a time, corresponding to the current section. As I advanced through the talk, the active box darkened and the others

faded. The following graphic demonstrates how color shifts in a row of boxes can guide your audience through a multi-part structure.

"A vocation is found by looking outside yourself and asking what problem is addressed by the activity you intrinsically enjoy."

- David Brooks

This method reinforces the structure without requiring extra text or symbols.

Add a Tracker to Your Content Slides

Wait until you've finalized the structure of your presentation before adding trackers. This ensures you won't have to redo them if slides are added, deleted, or rearranged.

Don't build trackers into your slide master. Because trackers represent different sections, you can't customize them slide by slide if they're built into the slide master. Adding them manually allows you to tailor the tracker for each section.

Once you've decided on the placement and format, the process to add trackers is quick and easy:

1. Create the tracker on the first content slide of a section.
2. Copy the tracker, go to the next slide, and paste it. The tracker will appear in the exact location.

3. Repeat this process for each slide in the section.

4. When you reach the first content slide of the next section, update the tracker to reflect the new section, and repeat.

Trackers can be tricky to get right. The table below shows a few common problems and what to do instead.

Tracker Issues

Issue	Recommendation
The tracker includes items that shouldn't be included on a tracker like "Introduction" "Agenda" or "Q&A."	Limit trackers to your main section or points.
The tracker is in an unconventional location (e.g., left or right margin).	Place the tracker on the lower-right corner of a slide, upper-right corner, in the top header, or the bottom footer.
The tracker text is difficult to read.	The size of text used within a tracker should be smaller than the body slide text, typically between 10 and 20 points, depending on how your deck will be consumed.
The tracker is too big.	Design the tracker so it doesn't compete with the main message of the slide.
The tracker text is a different font.	Use the same font as the body text.
The tracker distracts from the message.	Avoid unprofessional clip art. If using icons, ensure they are from the same family.
The tracker doesn't highlight the section.	Emphasize your current section using bold text, color, and/or shape.
The tracker is placed on Section-Divider Slides.	Omit from Section-Divider Slides because these are navigational aids themselves (the tracker becomes redundant).

Done well, trackers should feel like they belong on the slide and be helpful to your audience.

Application of Design Principles

To check that your deck consistently applies design principles throughout, consider these features:

- **Alignment:** Are headings and subheadings aligned consistently from slide to slide? Headings should always stay in the same position.
- **Proximity:** Are related elements grouped similarly on all slides? Charts and their captions should always appear in the same relative position.
- **Contrast:** Are you using the same styling across slides to signal hierarchy? If segment headings are placed in a colored box with white text on one slide, then consider formatting them the same way throughout.
- **Repetition:** Are font types, font sizes, color treatments, line spacing, bullet point size and style consistent across all slides? Consistent placement of slide elements also contributes to visual coherence.
- **White space:** Are margins and spacing between elements consistent throughout? Watch for slides that feel crowded compared to others. They may signal a need to add white space.

Maintain Consistent Slide Margins

Because presentation software doesn't include preset margins like word-processing software does, you'll need to manage the margin manually to maintain consistent white space. Without white space, content can feel crowded. As you review your deck, look for consistent margin use across slides:

- Check that each slide leaves similar space around the top, bottom, and sides.

- Avoid placing text or graphics in the margins, except for foot-notes or slide numbers.
- Aim for a picture-frame effect, where each slide feels intention-ally bordered by white space.

Remember: The white space created by margins provides visual relief for your audience.

Although each slide should make sense on its own, the entire set of slides should give the impression that it was built by the same person (even if many people contributed to the deck).

Assess the Text

If your deck is a story, your text is the narrator. Inconsistent tone, point of view, or language breaks the reader's trust, just like storytellers do when they change their voice mid-sentence.

Even the best-designed slides can be undermined by careless text. In the final stage of polishing, take time to review the text of your entire deck carefully, because inconsistent phrasing and formatting can weaken your message and hurt your credibility.

Start by stepping away from your screen. Print your deck. Read it slowly. The hard copy, and the slow read, makes it easier to notice incon-sistencies in tone, phrasing, or formatting that are harder to catch when you click quickly from slide to slide.

If possible, ask a colleague to review your printed deck and flag any-thing that's unclear, redundant, or inconsistent. Because you may have been working on the content for days or even weeks, you're likely to miss small issues. A fresh pair of eyes can help.

As you, and/or your colleague, review your deck, focus on language consistency, tone and point of view, formatting and grammar, and con-trast and readability.

Language Consistency

Be sure you're using terms consistently throughout the deck. Especially in collaborative decks, variation can muddle meaning. Some organizations have style guides to help maintain consistency.

For example, if one slide refers to "employees," and another says, "team members," and a third uses "associates," your audience may wonder whether those terms refer to different groups. Choose a term and use it consistently, especially for key roles, metrics, or concepts.

Tone and Point of View

Make sure that the tone and point of view are consistent throughout. Are you using formal or informal language, and does it match the audience's expectations? For internal decks, first-person references like "we," "us," or "our" can work well to signal shared ownership. But when writing for a client or external audience, a more formal tone may be appropriate. Whatever approach you choose, first person or third, apply it consistently.

Formatting and Grammar

Check sentence-level elements:

- Have you avoided double spaces after periods?
- Is your punctuation consistent (especially dashes, quotation marks, and commas)?
- Are same-level headings capitalized consistently?

Contrast and Readability

If you're unsure whether you have built in enough contrast between the text and background, print a slide or two in grayscale. If the words are difficult to read, consider adjusting the colors.

If you have access to the location where the deck will be presented, consider testing there as well. Sometimes the contrast on your screen will be very different from the contrast on a projector or television.

■ ■ ■

Remember: Your deck is a story. When structure, design, and language align across slides, your message becomes a narrative. And narrative is what your audience will remember and act on.

Chapter 10 Takeaways

- Even a strong slide can fall flat if it doesn't fit the bigger story. Step back and make sure your deck builds logically from start to finish.

- Read your slide headings in sequence. They should tell a clear, coherent story, even without the graphics or supporting text.

- Consistency builds trust. Fonts, colors, layouts, margins, and phrasing should be aligned throughout the deck.

- You don't need to force variety or uniformity. Choose the best layout for each idea, but make sure repeated elements (like section dividers) are styled consistently.

- Trackers are optional—but helpful. Use visual cues to help audiences stay oriented in longer or multipart presentations.

- Design principles apply across slides, not just within them. Check that alignment, proximity, contrast, white space, and repetition are working together from slide to slide.

- Margins matter. Slide software doesn't create them for you, so check that every slide includes intentional breathing room around the edges.

- Copy edit for consistency, clarity, and tone. Use the same terms, formatting styles, and grammatical structure across your deck to avoid distractions and build credibility.

Before we close, let's consider how to carry these principles into your next slide deck and beyond.

FINAL THOUGHTS

Better slide decks lead to clearer communication.

That's the central idea behind *Build Better Slide Decks.* When you take the time to plan with care, produce thoughtfully, and polish intentionally, you're doing more than formatting slides. You're shaping how others understand your ideas.

A well-made deck brings structure to complexity. It sharpens your message, guides your audience, and builds understanding. It turns scattered thoughts into a story that flows. When your slides are clear, people can follow your logic, see your main point, and grasp the details.

When design and structure are working well, they stay in the background. The story comes through. Your audience remembers the message. That's the invisible craft at work. The slides support the story rather than distract from it.

The value of these skills extends beyond your own decks. You now have tools to help others improve theirs. You can ask, What's the main point here? You can offer more constructive feedback. You can help someone turn a dense report into a compelling narrative or reorganize a cluttered slide into something clear. When you do, you elevate the way ideas get shared and understood.

Build Better Slide Decks was written with this goal in mind: to help you create sharper slides, stronger stories, and standout presentations.

You don't need to wait for the perfect project. Pick a deck, apply what you've learned, and make it better. One slide at a time, you'll raise the bar for yourself and for the people you work with.

As you apply these ideas, I hope this book continues to be a useful guide—one you can return to whenever you're shaping a new message or mentoring someone through theirs.

I'd love to hear how you're putting these ideas into practice. If this book helped you rethink a slide, improve a story, or guide your team through a deck, send me a note. And if you're interested in bringing this approach to your organization—whether through a virtual session, in-person workshop, or something custom—I'd be glad to talk. You can learn more at SlideDeckBook.com.

ACKNOWLEDGMENTS

This book would not have been possible without the love and support of my wife, Susanne, and our daughters, Grace and Sloan. They made space for this work in our lives, and they're the constant behind everything I do.

I'm grateful to my family for their steady encouragement throughout this project. My dad had a favorite check-in: "How many words did you write today?" My mom has long supported my writing habit and has been a generous feedback provider for my blog posts. My brother, Tyler, showed sincere interest at every step.

My interest in visual communication began as an undergraduate student at the Rochester Institute of Technology. Professor Diane Hope first helped me see the world through a visual lens, and her influence has shaped the way I think about communication to this day.

Teaching at RIT deepened my understanding of how visual thinking could enhance business communication. The talented students I worked with, especially Justin Thorp, Lauren Shapiro, and Nikesh Hajari, helped shape my early thinking.

At Cornell University, I've been fortunate to work alongside exceptional colleagues, including Daphne Jameson, Amy Newman, David Lennox, and Maria Wolfe. They were helpful thought partners as I learned how to guide my students through the process of crafting high-density decks.

My colleague and friend Craig Snow has had the greatest impact on this book. Craig helped me rework a course guide on high-density decks and co-developed the Plan–Produce–Polish framework for workshops we deliver together, which I later used to structure this book. He also contributed ideas that shaped the chapter on structure. He was the first reader of the full manuscript, and his thoughtful feedback made this a better book.

I'm grateful to the many Cornell students who shaped this work, including Ashley Zilenziger, Cassandra Rampino, Kayti Stanley, Nicholas Nelson, Samay Bansal, and the course assistants for my persuasive communication course. Your insights and feedback helped refine both the ideas and how I teach them.

The idea for this book took shape in collaboration with Vikki (Vaswani) Malhotra, a former student who was then a graduate student at Columbia. Our partnership in 2021 led to a comprehensive study of investor slide decks. Since then, two independent studies with Roberto Teran, a graduate student in Cornell's Baker Program in Real Estate, helped me analyze decks in new ways. Another independent study with Rachel Perry challenged me to think more rigorously about how we measure information density.

My thinking was further shaped by members of the Association for Business Communication, including Andy Spackman, Barbara Shwom, Lisa Gueldenzoph Snyder, Patricia Harms, and many others who continue to elevate our field.

I'm also thankful for the authors whose work influenced me long before I began writing this book: Barbara Minto, Bruce Gabrielle, Dan Roam, Edward Tufte, Gene Zelazny, Mary Munter, and Nancy Duarte. Their books, and the ideas within them, are woven throughout these pages. I'm especially lucky to have authors in my life who helped me believe I could be one too. Amy Newman and Neil Tarallo have offered encouragement at key moments along the way. I'm also grateful to Bruce Austin and Jim Fleming, whose support and example continue to influence me.

Finally, thank you to the team who helped bring this book across the finish line: Laura Boyle, Joe Peirson, Alan Barnett, Maria Sosnowski, Sandra Wendel, and Melanie Hoftyzer.

To everyone mentioned here, and to those who shaped this book in quieter ways, thank you for your part in bringing this book to life.

NOTES

Introduction

1. The term *slide deck* comes from the days of physical slide projectors, when presenters would load individual 35mm slides into a carousel or stack them like a deck of cards. When PowerPoint and other digital tools took over, the name stuck because just like a deck of cards, a slide deck is a collection of individual slides meant to be viewed in sequence.

    In this book, I will consistently use the term *slides* to refer to the individual elements of a presentation deck. While slides are typically presented and pages are read, I will use slides for both purposes to make guidance easier to follow, whether you are creating a deck to present or to read.

2. Edward R. Tufte, *The Cognitive Style of PowerPoint: Pitching Out Corrupts Within* (Cheshire, CT: Graphics Press, 2003).

3. Amazon, *2022 Shareholder Letter*, accessed February 6, 2025, https://s2.q4cdn.com/299287126/files/doc_financials/annual/Amazon_Shareholder_Letter.pdf.

4. Companies were using transparencies to present visuals as far back as the late 1950s. (A transparency is a clear plastic sheet that is placed on a glass surface, where a bright light and mirror system projects content onto a wall.) When PowerPoint was first released in 1987, it was designed to produce black-and-white transparencies. Users would print their slides on transparent sheets, which were then used with overhead projectors during presentations. For a brief history of the business presentations, read, JoAnne Yates and Wanda Orlikowski, "The PowerPoint Presentation and Its Corollaries: How Genres Shape Communicative Action in Organizations," *Communications of the ACM 50*, no. 4 (2007): 80–87.

5. According to a 2004 survey by the National Investor Relations Institute, the vast majority of companies represented by its members conducted conference calls, and nearly all of those calls were webcast. Source: National Investor Relations Institute, *Standards of Practice for Investor Relations* (Vienna, VA: NIRI, 2004), https://media.corporate-ir.net/media_files/priv/27585/standards_practice.pdf.

6. As far back as 2007, Management Communication scholars found that slide decks were being used for multiple, conflicting purposes (to support presentations, leave-behinds, and hybrid documents). Yates and Orlikowski suggested that, until clearer expectations about how slide decks should be used in different contexts, we can expect to see continued experimentation and communication challenges.

Part I

1. Wouter Kool, Joseph T. McGuire, Zev B. Rosen, and Matthew M. Botvinick, "Decision Making and the Avoidance of Cognitive Demand," *Journal of Experimental Psychology: General* 139, no. 4 (2010): 665–682.

Chapter 2

1. Stephen R. Covey, *The 7 Habits of Highly Effective People: Powerful Lessons in Personal Change*, rev. ed. (New York: Free Press, 2004).

2. Robert B. Cialdini, *Influence: The New Psychology of Modern Persuasion* (New York: Morrow, 1984).

3. Daniel Kahneman and Amos Tversky, "Prospect Theory: An Analysis of Decision under Risk," in *Handbook of the Fundamentals of Financial Decision Making: Part I*, eds. Leonard C. MacLean and William T. Ziemba (Singapore: World Scientific, 2013), 99–127.

4. Everett M. Rogers, Arvind Singhal, and Margaret M. Quinlan, "Diffusion of Innovations," in *An Integrated Approach to Communication Theory and Research*, eds. Don W. Stacks and Michael B. Salwen, 2nd ed. (New York: Routledge, 2014), 432–448.

5. Daniel Kahneman, *Thinking, Fast and Slow* (New York: Farrar, Straus and Giroux, 2011).

6. Uses and Gratifications Theory was first developed by Jay G. Blumler and Elihu Katz. See Jay G. Blumler and Elihu Katz, eds., *The Uses of Mass Communications: Current Perspectives on Gratifications Research* (Beverly Hills, CA: Sage, 1974). For a modern overview and application of the theory in contemporary media contexts, see Thomas E. Ruggiero, "Uses and Gratifications Theory in the 21st Century," *Mass Communication & Society* 3, no. 1 (2000): 3–37.

7. Richard E. Petty and John T. Cacioppo, "The Elaboration Likelihood Model of Persuasion," in *Advances in Experimental Social Psychology*, vol. 19, ed. Leonard Berkowitz (New York: Academic Press, 1986), 123–205, https://doi.org/10.1016/S0065-2601(08)60214-2.

8. Susanne G. Scott and Reginald A. Bruce, "Decision-Making Style: The Development and Assessment of a New Measure," *Educational and Psychological Measurement* 55, no. 5 (1995): 818–831, https://doi.org/10.1177/0013164495055005017.

9. Kittie W. Watson, Larry L. Barker, and James B. Weaver III, "The Listening Styles Profile (LSP-16): Development and Validation of an Instrument to Assess Four Listening Styles," *International Journal of Listening* 9, no. 1 (1995): 1–13, https://doi.org/10.1080/10904018.1995.10499138.

10. Hyunjin Song and Norbert Schwarz, "If It's Hard to Read, It's Hard to Do: Processing Fluency Affects Effort Prediction and Motivation," *Psychological Science* 19, no. 10 (2008): 986–988, https://doi.org/10.1111/j.1467-9280.2008.02189.x.

11. Chip Heath and Dan Heath, *Made to Stick: Why Some Ideas Survive and Others Die* (New York: Random House, 2007).

12. Tal Eyal, Mary L. Steffel, and Nicholas Epley, "Perspective Mistaking: Accurately Understanding the Mind of Another Requires Getting Perspective, Not Taking Perspective," *Journal of Personality and Social Psychology* 114, no. 4 (2018): 547–571.

Chapter 3

1. My thinking on structure has been strongly influenced by the work of Craig Snow, whose teaching and writing helped shape the framework that follows. What you'll see in this section is an applied adaptation of his ideas, tailored to slide decks. Craig R. Snow, *Four Cornerstones, Part III: Structuring Longer, More-Challenging, and More-Complex Documents* (unpublished course handout, Cornell University, November 15, 2024).

2. Barbara Minto, *The Pyramid Principle: Logic in Writing and Thinking*, 3rd ed. (Harlow, England: Financial Times Prentice Hall, 2010).

3. Bennet B. Murdock Jr., "The Serial Position Effect of Free Recall," *Journal of Experimental Psychology* 64, no. 5 (1962): 482–488, https://doi.org/10.1037/h0045106.

4. The SCR (Situation–Complication–Resolution) framework is adapted from the SCQA (Situation–Complication–Question–Answer) structure presented in Barbara Minto's *The Pyramid Principle*. While Minto primarily uses SCQA to frame problems and introductions, the core logic—introducing a situation, highlighting a complication, and then providing a resolution or key answer—is also fundamental to narrative structure.

Chapter 4

1. As Bruce Gabrielle puts it, "a chunk is anything your vision can see as part of a group and separate from other groups." See Bruce Gabrielle, *Speaking PowerPoint: The New Language of Business* (Seattle: Insights Publishing, 2010).

2. In a study I conducted with Roberto Teran, where we analyzed over 900 individual real-world slides, we found that close to 50% of the sample followed one of the three pairings in the table: low word count with low information chunk, medium word count with medium information chunk, or high word count with high information chunk. Mixed combinations were less common. For instance, a slide with low word count and high information chunk might include several concise chunks, which *can be* effective. The least common combination was high word count with low information chunk, which often results in dense, wall-to-wall text covering a single idea, a format that tends to reduce clarity. See Andrew B. Quagliata and Roberto A. Teran, "Are My Slides Too Busy? Measuring the Information Density of Workplace Slide Decks" (paper presented at the 88th Annual International Conference of the Association for Business Communication, Denver, CO, October 2023).

3. The example slides in this book are designed in grayscale. Most slide content can be made clear and effective without relying on color. For those interested in learning more about color, the *polishing* section of this book offers a variety of suggestions for drawing attention to key elements.

4. When a deck needs to serve both as a visual aid during a presentation and as a stand-alone resource, medium-density slides offer the most optimal balance. I've even advocated this approach to other communication professionals and educators, encouraging them to prioritize medium-density decks when teaching or designing for professional business contexts. See Andrew B. Quagliata, "Discussion Decks: Bridging the Gap Between What Business Communication Faculty Teach and What Industry Requires of Our Students" (paper presented at the Europe, Africa, and Middle East Regional Conference of the Association for Business Communication, Naples, Italy, January 2023).

Chapter 5

1. These terms appear in a range of published and professional sources. "Conclusion title" is used in Bruce Gabrielle, *Speaking PowerPoint*, 103. "Message titles" appear in Mary Munter and Lynn Russell, *Guide to Presentations* (Upper Saddle River, NJ: Pearson Education, 2002). "Sentence headers" are described in Traci Nathans-Kelly and Christine G. Nicometo, *Slide Rules: Design, Build, and Archive Presentations in*

the Engineering and Technical Fields (Hoboken, NJ: IEEE-Wiley, 2014). "Sentence headline" is the term used by Michael Alley and Kathryn Neeley in "Rethinking the Design of Presentation Slides: A Case for Sentence Headlines and Visual Evidence," *Technical Communication* 52, no. 4 (2005): 417–426. "Action titles" and "callouts" are common terms in consulting firm slide templates and internal training, though they are less frequently documented in publicly available materials.

2. Cliff Atkinson, *Beyond Bullet Points: Using Microsoft PowerPoint to Create Presentations That Inform, Motivate, and Inspire* (Redmond, WA: Microsoft Press, 2005).

3. Gene Zelazny, *Say It with Presentations: How to Design and Deliver Successful Business Presentations* (New York: McGraw-Hill, 2000).

4. Mary Munter, *Guide to Managerial Communication* (Prentice Hall, 2012).

5. This finding is supported by research on the assertion-evidence approach, which advocates using full-sentence slide headlines ("assertions") paired with visual evidence. See Joanna Garner and Michael Alley, "How the Design of Presentation Slides Affects Audience Comprehension: A Case for the Assertion-Evidence Approach," *International Journal of Engineering Education* 29, no. 6 (2013): 1564–1579.

6. Dave McKinsey, *Strategic Storytelling: How to Create Persuasive Business Presentations* (independently published, 2014).

Chapter 6

1. Atkinson, *Beyond Bullet Points.*

2. Zelazny, *Say It with Presentations.*

3. Garr Reynolds, *Presentation Zen: Simple Ideas on Presentation Design and Delivery* (Berkeley, CA: New Riders, 2011).

4. While *visual* is a broader term than *graphic*, it can also include text, which is inherently visual in form. To avoid confusion, I use the term *graphic* throughout this book when referring specifically to images, charts, and graphs.

5. Ralph N. Haber, "How We Remember What We See," *Scientific American* 222, no. 5 (1970): 104–115.

6. Allan Paivio, *Mental Representations: A Dual Coding Approach* (New York: Oxford University Press, 1986).

7. In researching this book, I came across many claims that the brain processes images 60,000 times faster than text, but I could find no scientific evidence to support that number. What research does show is that people can recognize visual stimuli in as little as 150 milliseconds,

according to Simon Thorpe, Denis Fize, and Catherine Marlot in their 1996 *Nature* article, "Speed of Processing in the Human Visual System." Text, on the other hand, takes roughly 150 to 300 milliseconds to process depending on word frequency, predictability, and complexity, as reported by Reinhold Kliegl, Antje Nuthmann, and Ralf Engbert in their 2006 article, "Tracking the Mind During Reading," published in the *Journal of Experimental Psychology: General*.

8. Douglas L. Nelson, Valerie S. Reed, and James R. Walling, "Pictorial Superiority Effect," *Journal of Experimental Psychology: Human Learning and Memory* 2, no. 5 (1976): 523–528, https://doi.org/10.1037/0278-7393.2.5.523.

9. Terry L. Childers and Michael J. Houston, "Conditions for a Picture-Superiority Effect on Consumer Memory," *Journal of Consumer Research* 11, no. 2 (1984): 643–654, https://doi.org/10.1086/208990.

10. John Medina, *Brain Rules: 12 Principles for Surviving and Thriving at Work, Home, and School* (Seattle: Pear Press, 2008).

11. Dan Roam, *Blah Blah: What to Do When Words Don't Work* (New York: Penguin, 2011).

12. Quagliata and Teran, "Are My Slides Too Busy?"

13. Allan Paivio, *Imagery and Verbal Processes* (New York: Holt, Rinehart and Winston, 1971).

14. Anne Treisman, "Preattentive Processing in Vision," *Computer Vision, Graphics, and Image Processing* 31, no. 2 (1985): 156–177, https://doi.org/10.1016/S0734-189X(85)80004-9.

15. Anne M. Treisman and Garry Gelade, "A Feature-Integration Theory of Attention," *Cognitive Psychology* 12, no. 1 (1980): 97–136, https://doi.org/10.1016/0010-0285(80)90005-5.

16. John Sweller, "Cognitive Load During Problem Solving: Effects on Learning," *Cognitive Science* 12, no. 2 (1988): 257–285, https://doi.org/10.1207/s15516709cog1202_4.

17. Barbara Tversky, "Structures of Mental Spaces: How People Think About Space," *Environment and Behavior* 35, no. 1 (2003): 66–80, https://doi.org/10.1177/0013916502238865.

18. Jean Piaget, *The Origins of Intelligence in Children*, trans. Margaret Cook (New York: International Universities Press, 1952).

19. I'm grateful to Rachel Perry, who surfaced this insight during an independent study on automating the evaluation of slide deck density.

20. In a study I conducted with Vikki (Vaswani) Malhotra, we found that none of the publicly traded company slide decks in our sample included a reference or bibliography slide. See Andrew B. Quagliata and Vikki Vaswani, "State of Decking: How Public Companies Communicate Using Slide Decks" (paper presented at the 86th Annual International Conference of the Association for Business Communication, online, October 2021).

21. California State University, Chico, *Evaluating Information—Applying the CRAAP Test*, Meriam Library, accessed May 31, 2025, https://web .archive.org/web/20180508150205/http://libguides.csuchico.edu/ c.php?g=414315&p=2822716.

Chapter 7

1. Alan Baddeley, "Working Memory," *Science* 255, no. 5044 (1992): 556–559, https://doi.org/10.1126/science.1736359.

2. Alexandre N. Tuch, Javier A. Bargas-Avila, Klaus Opwis, and Frank H. Wilhelm, "Visual Complexity of Websites: Effects on Users' Experience, Physiology, Performance, and Memory," *International Journal of Human-Computer Studies* 67, no. 9 (2009): 703–715, https://doi.org/10.1016/ j.ijhcs.2009.04.002.

3. This research refines George A. Miller's classic "seven, plus or minus two" rule, showing that our brains are wired to process fewer chunks than previously believed. See Nelson Cowan, "The Magical Number 4 in Short-Term Memory: A Reconsideration of Mental Storage Capacity," *Behavioral and Brain Sciences* 24, no. 1 (2001): 87–114, https://doi.org/10.1017/ S0140525X01003922; and George A. Miller, "The Magical Number Seven, Plus or Minus Two: Some Limits on Our Capacity for Processing Information," *Psychological Review* 63 (1956): 81–97.

4. Hugh Dubberly, "The 892 Unique Ways to Partition a 3 × 4 Grid," Dubberly Design Office, accessed February 21, 2025, https://www.dubberly.com/ concept-maps/3x4grid.html. The visualization was designed by Thomas Gaskin, with creative direction by Hugh Dubberly, algorithms by Patrick Kessler, and the original patent held by William Drenttel and Jessica Helfand.

5. This type of layout may seem to exceed the recommended four chunks per slide, but it reflects a design with sub-chunks. For example, a slide with three rows and six boxes may be organized as three primary chunks (the rows), each containing two related sub-chunks. As long as the grouping is visually clear, this kind of structure can work well—especially in medium- or high-density decks. To maintain clarity, aim to limit the number of sub-chunks within any one chunk to three or four.

6. Johan Wagemans, James H. Elder, Michael Kubovy, Stephen E. Palmer, Mary A. Peterson, Manish Singh, and Rüdiger von der Heydt, "A Century of Gestalt Psychology in Visual Perception I. Perceptual Grouping and Figure–Ground Organization," *Psychological Bulletin* 138, no. 6 (2012): 1172–1217, https://doi.org/10.1037/a0029333.

7. Quagliata and Teran, "Are My Slides Too Busy?"

8. Nancy Duarte, *slide:ology: The Art and Science of Creating Great Presentations* (Sebastopol, CA: O'Reilly Media, 2008).

Chapter 8

1. Daniel H. Pink, *To Sell Is Human: The Surprising Truth about Moving Others* (New York: Penguin, 2013).

Chapter 9

1. Edward R. Tufte, *The Visual Display of Quantitative Information* (Cheshire, CT: Graphics Press, 1983).

2. For an accessible introduction to core design principles—contrast, repetition, alignment, and proximity—see Robin Williams, *The Non-Designer's Design Book*, 4th ed. (San Francisco: Peachpit Press, 2014). Her book offers a useful foundation for improving visual layout and design, especially for those without formal design training.

3. World Wide Web Consortium (W3C). *Web Content Accessibility Guidelines (WCAG) 2.2.* W3C Recommendation, October 5, 2023. https://www.w3.org/TR/WCAG22/.

4. This guidance might remind you of the 4x4 or 5x5 slide rules. But I'm not advocating rigid formulas. Instead, I'm offering these ranges to guide your text layout decisions with audience cognition in mind. Unlike oversimplified rules that often ignore content and context, these recommendations are grounded in research about how people read and process visual information.

5. Steven J. Muncer, Bernard S. Gorman, Shepard Gorman, and Daniel Bibel. "Right Is Wrong: An Examination of the Effect of Right Justification on Reading," *British Journal of Educational Technology* 17, no. 1 (1986): 5–10, https://doi.org/10.1111/j.1467-8535.1986.tb00491.x.

6. Title case not only takes more time to apply but also tends to confuse people about which words count as "major." As a general rule, major words include nouns, pronouns, verbs, adjectives, adverbs, and subordinating conjunctions (like *because* or *although*). Minor words—typically not capitalized unless they appear first or last—include articles

(*a, an, the*), coordinating conjunctions (*and, but, or*), and prepositions (*in, on, with*). If your organization requires title case, consider using a title case checker or following a style guide such as *The Chicago Manual of Style* or *AP Stylebook* for consistency.

7. Dan Roam, *The Back of the Napkin: Solving Problems and Selling Ideas with Pictures* (New York: Portfolio, 2008).

8. Gene Zelazny, *Say It with Charts: The Executive's Guide to Visual Communication*, 4th ed. (New York: McGraw-Hill, 2001).

9. Nancy Duarte, "Make Your Data Insights Visually Consumable," *MIT Sloan Management Review*, October 5, 2020, https://sloanreview.mit.edu/article/make-your-data-insights-visually-consumable/.

INDEX

ABOUT THE AUTHOR

Andrew B. Quagliata, PhD, teaches management communication at Cornell University and leads Ethos Communication Advisors, where he delivers training for some of the world's most respected companies.

He is the author of four eCornell courses, including *Building Compelling Slide Decks and Reports, Developing Self-Advocacy Skills, Generative AI for Written Communication,* and *Preparing for Effective Presentations Using AI*. Andrew chairs the Teaching Committee for the Association for Business Communication and received the association's Rising Star Award in 2019. At Cornell, he has earned numerous teaching awards. Since 2018, Andrew has posted more than 100 articles related to leadership communication at www.andrewquagliata.com, where he also shares free resources with his newsletter subscribers. He lives in Ithaca, New York, with his wife and their two daughters.

For information about training workshops and keynotes, visit www.andrewquagliata.com.